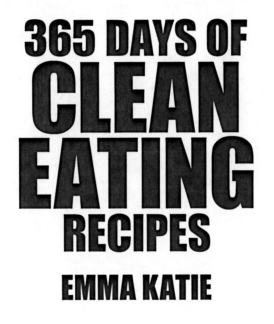

365 DAYS OF CLEAN EATING RECIPES

EMMA KATIE

Check out more books by Emma Katie at:
www.amazon.com/author/emmakatie

CONTENTS

Breakfast Recipes

Lunch Recipes

Dinner Recipes

Dessert Recipes

INTRODUCTION

Mounting evidence has shown that we are born with more chemicals in our bodies than we should have. And what do we do as we grow up?! We ingest even more of those chemicals, whether through water, air or the food choices we make. The toxicity often manifests in ways we may not understand or even know the source. It could be heart problems, obesity, diabetes, and the list goes on. Almost every health problem has one foundation – how toxic we are on the inside.

We call it progress but here's the irony of it all – progress should be good for us. Instead, for many years, the food industry used more chemicals and additives and called it progress. The way our grandmothers or great-grandmothers used to cook or preserve food was no longer considered reliable, healthy or nutritious. We were bombarded with commercials about chemicals that supposedly improved the taste of our food. We would rejoice on tasting simple things like garden tomatoes that had become a rare treat.

In recent years, demand has been growing for natural, healthy food, though too many people still succumb to the unhealthy temptation of overly processed fast food and convenience food. Solutions can be found and if you really want it, healthy eating is possible. Sure, it's more time consuming, it may be more expensive, but at the end of the day it means investing in your own health!

DEFINITION

Clean eating has known many definitions through the years and they all come from how people define the word "clean." Body builders have one definition, your food coach has another, a vegan can surely come up with a different one, and your doctor will find a new way to define the word as well. At the end of the day, though, the truth is somewhere in between so let's look at the facts and draw our own conclusions:

- Clean eating is not a diet.
- A diet often defines a period of time that has certain food restrictions with the sole purpose of losing weight or fixing a health problem. A diet is short-term thinking and it provides a short-term fix. But clean eating is quite the opposite – it has to become a lifestyle for it to work, focusing on a long-term purpose rather than seeing just the short-term benefits.
- There are no calorie restrictions. We all know how annoying, frustrating and time-consuming counting calories can be, but clean eating has none of this. Instead, it allows you to eat as much as you want and need to be healthy and have enough energy to do your daily tasks.
- There is no food deprivation. How many times have you been on a diet forbidding you to eat a certain food, ruling out your favorite meat or vegetable, and not even thinking about dessert?! Far too many times! And it's time to change that! Clean eating is not supposed to be a sacrifice or a chore. It's about finding healthy alternatives to unhealthy food. Let's say you love cake – why

give it up?! You can easily find a healthier alternative and enjoy it as much as you would with any other cake!

- You can eat as many times a day as you want. No more eating at certain hours or counting the minutes until you can have another tiny snack. Clean eating doesn't focus on that – it's your personal choice how many meals a day you have as long as they are healthy and packed with nutrients, not just calories to keep you full.
- Guidelines are not rules. Unlike diets, clean eating doesn't have strict rules. Instead, it has what I call guidelines – they are there just to guide you and teach you how to live a healthier life, instead of forcing you to comply with rules, which we all know never works!

CLEAN EATING GUIDELINES

✓ Avoid processed foods – they are usually high in additives and chemicals, salt and refined sugar, and that's not something you want in your system.

✓ Avoid refined foods – this includes refined flour, sugars and fats. Cutting these down in your diet will produce weight loss and correct insulin levels at the same time.

✓ Avoid alcohol – alcohol goes into the blood which then goes into your system, disturbing the way your liver, heart and kidneys work, so alcohol is definitely not something you want to drink. However, if you do go out and have to drink, keep it on a very low level.

✓ Avoid preservatives – read the labels of each food you buy and if it has ingredients that you can barely pronounce, don't buy it! As simple as that!

✓ Avoid artificial sweeteners – refined sugar is a no-no, but so are artificial sweeteners, so don't fool yourself. As their name states, they are artificial, made by humans in a lab. There's nothing natural or healthy about them.

✓ You and your food needs are important – choose your foods wisely and tailor your eating habits to suit your needs, according to your health, your daily tasks, or cravings. Clean eating is a highly customizable lifestyle, keep that in mind all the time!

✓ Establish goals and eat accordingly – losing weight or gaining weight, fixing a health problem or preventing one, clean eating can make it happen!

✓ Veggies, veggies, veggies, that's the golden rule! Luckily, vegetables come in a wide variety so you'll never get bored of combining them into new and appealing dishes.

✓ Eat fruits in moderation – unlike vegetables, fruits are sweet and the chance of eating too much and interfering with your goal is very high. Too much sugar leads to high blood sugar levels or interferes with your hormones.

✓ Eat high-quality ingredients – from meat to veggies and fruits, try picking the best ingredients you can afford. This doesn't mean eating expensive foods, but choosing wisely the ones that provide the most nutrients for their price.

✓ Eat healthy fats – fat is not the culprit for weight gain. In fact, fat is good for your brain. But always choose healthy fats – almonds, walnuts, chia seeds, avocados, eggs, extra virgin olive oil, coconut oil, good quality butter and grass-fed meat.

- ✓ Drink enough water – nothing beats pure, natural water in terms of what you drink. A glass of water early in the morning is the way to go for a clean, detoxified system.
- ✓ Use less salt when cooking and read labels to find the products that have less salt.
- ✓ Cut back on caffeine – one cup of coffee a day is okay for some people, but reducing it is a good idea if you have already have certain health problems.
- ✓ Find out what works for you personally and stick to it, but don't be afraid to step out of your comfort zone and discover new recipes, new ingredients, new flavor combinations.

Breakfast Recipes

Mixed Berry Smoothie

Time: 10 minutes

Servings: 4

Ingredients:

¼ cup blanched almonds
1 cup mixed berries
4 Medjool dates

2 cups coconut milk
1 tablespoon honey

Directions:

Combine all the ingredients in your blender.
Pulse until smooth and well blended.
Pour the drink in glasses and serve it right away.

Nutritional information per serving

Calories: 368
Fat: 31.7g

Protein: 4.8g
Carbohydrates: 27g

Tomato Sauce Poached Eggs

Time: 30 minutes

Servings: 4

Ingredients:

2 tablespoons extra virgin olive oil
1 shallot, sliced
2 garlic cloves, minced
1 cup tomato sauce
1 cup diced tomatoes

½ cup water
1 bay leaf
Salt and pepper to taste
4 eggs
2 tablespoons chopped parsley

Directions:

Heat oil in a frying pan and add the shallot and garlic. Cook for a few seconds then stir in the tomato sauce, tomatoes, water and bay leaf.
Season with salt and pepper and cook for 10 minutes on low heat.
Crack open the eggs and drop them in the hot sauce. Cook just for a few minutes until set.
Sprinkle with chopped parsley and serve right away.

Nutritional information per serving

Calories: 149
Fat: 11.6g

Protein: 6g
Carbohydrates: 6.9g

Spinach Omelet

Time: 25 minutes   Servings: 4

Ingredients:

2 tablespoons extra virgin olive oil
½ pound spinach, shredded

6 eggs, beaten
Salt and pepper to taste

Directions:

Heat oil in a skillet and add the spinach. Cook for a few minutes until softened.
Add the eggs, salt and pepper and cook for a few minutes on each side until set and golden.
Serve the omelet warm and fresh.

Nutritional information per serving

Calories: 168
Fat: 13.8g

Protein: 9.9g
Carbohydrates: 2.6g

Spicy Tomato Scrambled Eggs

Time: 25 minutes   Servings: 4

Ingredients:

2 tablespoons extra virgin olive oil
4 eggs, beaten
1 tomato, peeled and diced
½ jalapeño pepper, chopped

1 tablespoon grated Parmesan
1 tablespoon chopped cilantro
Salt and pepper to taste

Directions:

Heat the oil in a skillet or frying pan.
In a bowl, mix the eggs, tomato, pepper, Parmesan and cilantro then season with salt and pepper. Pour this mixture into the hot oil.
Cook for 2-3 minutes, stirring all the time, until the eggs are creamy and set.
Serve the eggs warm and fresh.

Nutritional information per serving

Calories: 136
Fat: 11.4g

Protein: 5.7g
Carbohydrates: 1.1g

Egg in a Bell Pepper Ring

Time: 10 minutes   Servings: 4

Ingredients:

1 red bell pepper
3 tablespoons extra virgin olive oil

4 eggs
Salt and pepper to taste

Directions:

Cut the bell peppers into thin rings.

Heat the olive oil in a frying pan.

Place the rings in the hot oil then crack open the eggs and drop them inside the pepper rings. Add salt and pepper to taste.

Fry until set and serve the eggs warm.

Nutritional information per serving

Calories: 162

Fat: 15g

Protein: 5.8g

Carbohydrates: 2.1g

Mozzarella Baked Eggs

Time: 15 minutes

Servings: 2

Ingredients:

2 tablespoons extra virgin olive oil

1 red bell pepper, cored and diced

¼ jalapeño chopped

2 oz. mozzarella, shredded

2 eggs

Salt and pepper to taste

Directions:

Grease 2 ramekins with olive oil then spoon bell pepper, jalapeño and mozzarella in each ramekin.

Crack open the eggs and drop them into each ramekin. Season with salt and pepper.

Cook in the preheated oven at 350F for 5-7 minutes.

Serve the eggs warm and fresh.

Nutritional information per serving

Calories: 283

Fat: 23.6g

Protein: 14.2g

Carbohydrates: 5g

Spiced Banana Smoothie

Time: 10 minutes

Servings: 2

Ingredients:

1 banana

2 tablespoons almond butter

¼ teaspoon cinnamon powder

1 pinch ground ginger

2 tablespoons hemp seeds

2 tablespoons honey

1 cup coconut milk

Directions:

Combine all the ingredients in a blender and pulse until smooth.

Pour the drink into serving glasses and drink it fresh and chilled.

Nutritional information per serving

Calories: 436
Fat: 41.3g

Protein: 9.3g
Carbohydrates: 40.8g

Muesli Blueberry Smoothie Bowl

Time: 15 minutes

Servings: 3

Ingredients:

1 cup fresh blueberries
1 teaspoon lemon zest
1 teaspoon lemon juice

1 cup almond milk
2 tablespoons raw honey
1 cup muesli

Directions:

Combine the blueberries, lemon zest, lemon juice, almond milk and honey in a blender and pulse until smooth.
Pour the smoothie into 2 bowls and top with muesli.
Serve the bowls warm and fresh.

Nutritional information per serving

Calories: 357
Fat: 21g

Protein: 5g
Carbohydrates: 44.5g

Cinnamon Carrot Baked Oatmeal

Time: 20 minutes

Servings: 6

Ingredients:

2 cups rolled oats
¼ teaspoon cinnamon powder
¼ teaspoon ground ginger
½ cup walnuts, chopped
2 carrots, grated

¼ cup maple syrup
¼ cup dates, pitted and chopped
2 cups coconut milk
2 tablespoons raw honey

Directions:

Combine all the ingredients in a deep dish baking pan.
Cook in the preheated oven at 350F for 10-15 minutes until softened.
Serve the oatmeal warm or chilled.

Nutritional information per serving

Calories: 437
Fat: 27.1g

Protein: 8.3g
Carbohydrates: 46.1g

OVERNIGHT CHIA PUDDING

Time: 12 hours   Servings: 4

Ingredients:

1 banana
2 tablespoons cocoa powder
2 tablespoons rolled oats

1 ½ cups coconut milk
2 tablespoons honey
3 tablespoons chia seeds

Directions:

Combine the banana, cocoa powder, oats, coconut milk and honey in a blender and pulse until smooth.
Add the chia seeds and mix well then pour in a bowl and place in the fridge overnight.
Serve the puddings chilled.

Nutritional information per serving

Calories: 398   Protein: 8g
Fat: 29.3g   Carbohydrates: 31.5g

PAPAYA ACAI BOWL

Time: 25 minutes   Servings: 4

Ingredients:

1 banana
1 cup blueberries
1 cup coconut milk
¼ cup water

2 tablespoons hemp seeds
2 tablespoons honey
1 papaya, peeled and cubed
¼ cup sliced almonds

Directions:

Combine the banana, blueberries, coconut milk, water, hemp seeds and honey in a blender and pulse
    until smooth.
Pour the mixture into bowls and top with papaya and sliced almonds.
Serve right away.

Nutritional information per serving

Calories: 306   Protein: 4.9g
Fat: 19.4g   Carbohydrates: 34g

HONEY OATMEAL PUDDING

Time: 20 minutes   Servings: 4

Ingredients:

1 cup water
1 cup coconut milk

1 cup rolled oats
¼ cup raw honey

½ teaspoon vanilla extract
1 pinch ground ginger

2 tablespoons ground flaxseeds

Directions:

Combine all the ingredients in a saucepan and place over low flame.
Cook for 10 minutes, stirring all the time, until the pudding is thickened.
Serve the pudding warm.

Nutritional information per serving

Calories: 300
Fat: 16.7g

Protein: 4.8g
Carbohydrates: 35.7g

Herbed Baked Eggs

Time: 15 minutes

Servings: 2

Ingredients:

2 tablespoons extra virgin olive oil
2 eggs

2 tablespoons chopped cilantro
Salt and pepper to taste

Directions:

Grease 2 ramekins with oil. Crack open the eggs and drop them in the ramekins.
Top with cilantro and season with salt and pepper.
Cook in the preheated oven at 350F for 5 minutes.
Serve the eggs warm and fresh.

Nutritional information per serving

Calories: 183
Fat: 18.4g

Protein: 5.6g
Carbohydrates: 0.4g

Mozzarella Sweet Potato Frittata

Time: 25 minutes

Servings: 4

Ingredients:

4 eggs, beaten
¼ teaspoon smoked paprika
¼ teaspoon dried oregano
Salt and pepper to taste

2 tablespoons extra virgin olive oil
2 sweet potatoes, peeled and diced
4 oz. mozzarella, shredded

Directions:

Mix the eggs, paprika, oregano, salt and pepper in a bowl.
Heat the oil in a frying pan. Add the sweet potatoes and cook for a few minutes on all sides.
Pour the eggs over the potatoes then lower the heat and cook for 5-10 minutes until set.
When done, top with shredded mozzarella and serve the frittata warm.

Nutritional information per serving

Calories: 293
Fat: 16.6g

Protein: 14.8g
Carbohydrates: 22.4g

Kale Egg Muffins

Time: 25 minutes

Servings: 12

Ingredients:

10 eggs, beaten
6 kale leaves, shredded
¼ teaspoon chili powder
Olive oil to grease the pan

Salt and pepper to taste
¼ cup coconut milk
1 cup shredded mozzarella

Directions:

Combine the eggs, kale, chili powder, salt and pepper, coconut milk and mozzarella in a bowl.
Grease a muffin tin with olive oil then pour the egg and kale mixture into each muffin cup.
Bake in the preheated oven at 350F for 10 minutes.
Serve the muffins warm or chilled.

Nutritional information per serving

Calories: 108
Fat: 5.9g

Protein: 8.4g
Carbohydrates: 4.4g

Green Creamy Spinach

Time: 20 minutes

Servings: 4

Ingredients:

2 tablespoons extra virgin olive oil
1 garlic clove, minced
2 cups baby spinach, shredded
4 kale leaves, shredded

4 eggs, beaten
1 pinch chili flakes
1 pinch dried oregano
Salt and pepper to taste

Directions:

Heat the oil in a frying pan or skillet and add the garlic. Cook for a few seconds until fragrant then add the spinach and kale and cook just until softened.
Add the eggs, chili flakes, oregano, salt and pepper and cook, mixing all the time, until creamy and thickened.
Serve the eggs warm and fresh.

Nutritional information per serving

Calories: 161
Fat: 11.4g

Protein: 8g
Carbohydrates: 8.2g

Cherry Breakfast Rice Bowls

Time: 30 minutes   Servings: 4

Ingredients:

⅔ cup brown rice, rinsed   2 tablespoons raw honey
½ cup rolled oats   1 pinch salt
1 ½ cups coconut milk   1 teaspoon grated lemon zest
1 cup water   2 cups fresh cherries, pitted

Directions:

Combine the rice, oats, coconut milk, water, honey, salt and lemon zest in a heavy saucepan.
Cook over low heat for 15-20 minutes until thickened and soft.
Pour the mixture into serving bowls and allow to cool down then top with fresh cherries and serve right
   away.

Nutritional information per serving

Calories: 399   Protein: 5.8g
Fat: 23g   Carbohydrates: 44.8g

Avocado Eggs Benedict

Time: 20 minutes   Servings: 4

Ingredients:

4 eggs   1 jalapeño, chopped
4 cups baby spinach   2 tablespoons extra virgin olive oil
1 avocado   Salt and pepper to taste
1 lemon, juiced

Directions:

Pour a few cups of water in a saucepan and bring it to the boil with a pinch of salt.
Crack open the eggs and drop them in the boiling water. Cook for 1 minute just until set then carefully
   drain.
Place the spinach on serving plates. Top each plate with poached eggs.
For the sauce, mix the avocado, lemon juice, jalapeño and olive oil, as well as salt and pepper in a blender.
   Pulse until smooth and creamy.
Spoon the sauce over the eggs and serve right away.

Nutritional information per serving

Calories: 232   Protein: 7.4g
Fat: 21.3g   Carbohydrates: 5.8g

Mixed Citrus Salad with Mint

Time: 20 minutes

Servings: 4

Ingredients:

2 grapefruits, cut into segments
2 oranges, cut into segments
1 blood orange, cut into segments

2 oranges, peeled and sliced
4 mint leaves, chopped
2 tablespoons raw honey

Directions:

Combine all the ingredients in a bowl and mix gently with a fork or spatula.
Serve the salad warm and fresh.

Nutritional information per serving

Calories: 161
Fat: 0.3g

Protein: 2.6g
Carbohydrates: 40.9g

Vegetarian Hash

Time: 30 minutes

Servings: 4

Ingredients:

3 tablespoons extra virgin olive oil
1 shallot, chopped
1 eggplant, peeled and cubed
1 sweet potato, peeled and diced
½ pound broccoli, cut into segments

¼ teaspoon dried oregano
½ teaspoon dried basil
Salt and pepper to taste
1 tablespoon balsamic vinegar

Directions:

Heat the oil in a frying pan or skillet. Add the shallot and cook for 1 minute then stir in the eggplant,
   sweet potato and broccoli.
Stir in the oregano and basil, as well as salt and pepper and cook for 10 minutes, stirring often.
Drizzle with balsamic vinegar and serve warm.

Nutritional information per serving

Calories: 165
Fat: 11g

Protein: 3.3g
Carbohydrates: 16.5g

Ricotta Spinach Frittata

Time: 30 minutes

Servings: 6

Ingredients:

1 cup ricotta cheese
4 eggs

½ teaspoon dried oregano
Salt and pepper to taste

2 cups baby spinach
1 pinch chili flakes

3 tablespoons extra virgin olive oil

Directions:

Mix the cheese, eggs, oregano, salt and pepper to taste in a bowl. Add the spinach and chili flakes.
Heat the oil in a frying pan or skillet then pour the egg mixture in the hot pan.
Lower the heat and cook for 10 minutes, turning it at least one time over to ensure even cooking.
Serve the ricotta warm and fresh.

Nutritional information per serving

Calories: 162
Fat: 13.2g

Protein: 8.8g
Carbohydrates: 2.8g

SPICED QUINOA FOR BREAKFAST

Time: 30 minutes

Servings: 4

Ingredients:

½ cup quinoa, rinsed
1 cup coconut milk
1 cup water
¼ teaspoon cinnamon powder

¼ teaspoon ground ginger
1 pinch nutmeg
2 tablespoons raw honey
¼ cup dried cranberries

Directions:

Combine the quinoa and the rest of the ingredients in a saucepan.
Cook on low heat for 20-25 minutes or until the liquid has been absorbed completely.
Serve the quinoa warm or chilled.

Nutritional information per serving

Calories: 253
Fat: 15.6g

Protein: 4.4g
Carbohydrates: 26.3g

DRIED FRUIT OATMEAL

Time: 35 minutes

Servings: 6

Ingredients:

1 ½ cups rolled oats
½ cup dried cranberries
¼ cup raisins
½ cup dried apricots, chopped
¼ cup dried pineapple, diced

1 ½ cups water
1 ½ cups coconut milk
2 tablespoons raw honey
1 pinch nutmeg
1 pinch salt

Directions:

Combine the oats with the rest of the ingredients in a saucepan.

Cook on low heat for 15-20 minutes or until thickened and soft.
Serve the oatmeal warm or chilled.

Nutritional information per serving

Calories: 270

Fat: 15.8g

Protein: 4.5g

Carbohydrates: 30.9g

SPICED GRANOLA

Time: 30 minutes

Servings: 6

Ingredients:

4 cups rolled oats
½ cup sliced almonds
½ cup walnuts, chopped
¼ cup pumpkin seeds
¼ teaspoon cinnamon powder

¼ teaspoon ground ginger
¼ teaspoon ground star anise
¼ teaspoon salt
½ cup maple syrup
¼ cup virgin coconut oil

Directions:

Combine the oats, almonds, walnuts and pumpkin seeds, as well as the spices and salt in a bowl.

Mix the coconut oil and maple syrup in a saucepan and melt them together over low heat. Pour the mixture over the dry ingredients and mix well.

Spread the mixture over a baking tray lined with parchment paper and bake in the preheated oven at 350F for 10 minutes.

Serve the granola chilled.

Nutritional information per serving

Calories: 498

Fat: 25.7g

Protein: 12.8g

Carbohydrates: 58.9g

ORANGE FLAXSEED SMOOTHIE

Time: 15 minutes

Servings: 2

Ingredients:

2 oranges, cut into segments
2 peaches, pitted and sliced
1 cup carrot juice

¼ teaspoon cinnamon powder
1 pinch ground ginger
2 tablespoons ground flaxseeds

Directions:

Combine all the ingredients in a blender. Pulse until smooth and creamy.
Serve the smoothie fresh and chilled.

Nutritional information per serving

Calories: 185

Fat: 2.7g

Protein: 4.4g

Carbohydrates: 38.5g

RASPBERRY PEACH SMOOTHIE BOWL

Time: 15 minutes   Servings: 4

Ingredients:

4 peaches, pitted and sliced   2 tablespoons hemp seeds
1 cup coconut milk   2 tablespoons raw honey
½ cup water   2 cups fresh raspberries

Directions:

Combine the peaches, coconut milk, water, hemp seeds and honey in a blender and pulse until smooth.
Pour the mixture into serving bowls and top with fresh raspberries.
Serve right away.

Nutritional information per serving

Calories: 271   Protein: 4.3g
Fat: 16.7g   Carbohydrates: 28.9g

GREEN MORNING SMOOTHIE

Time: 15 minutes   Servings: 2

Ingredients:

1 cucumber, sliced   1 cup coconut milk
2 kiwi fruits, peeled and sliced   2 tablespoons raw honey
1 cup baby spinach   1 pinch ground ginger

Directions:

Combine all the ingredients in a blender and pulse until smooth and creamy.
Pour the mixture into glasses and serve right away.

Nutritional information per serving

Calories: 413   Protein: 5.1g
Fat: 29.2g   Carbohydrates: 41g

CRANBERRY MUESLI GLASSES

Time: 30 minutes   Servings: 2

Ingredients:

1 cup rolled oats   1 cup low fat plain yogurt
¼ cup maple syrup   ¼ cup dried cranberries
¼ teaspoon cinnamon powder   1 cup fresh raspberries
2 tablespoons coconut oil, melted

Directions:

Mix the oats, maple syrup, cinnamon and coconut oil in a bowl.
Layer the yogurt, oat mixture and cranberries in serving glasses.
Top with plenty of fresh raspberries and serve the glasses fresh.

Nutritional information per serving

Calories: 434
Fat: 18g

Protein: 12.1g
Carbohydrates: 58.7g

MUSHROOM KALE HASH

Time: 25 minutes

Servings: 6

Ingredients:

3 tablespoons extra virgin olive oil
2 garlic cloves, minced
1 shallot, sliced
1 pound mushrooms, sliced

6 kale leaves, shredded
Salt and pepper to taste
1 tablespoon balsamic vinegar

Directions:

Heat the oil in a skillet or frying pan and add the garlic and shallot, as well as the mushrooms. Cook over low to medium heat for 5 minutes.
Stir in the kale leaves and season with salt and pepper.
Cook for a few more minutes until softened then add the vinegar and mix well.
Serve the hash warm and fresh.

Nutritional information per serving

Calories: 123
Fat: 7.2g

Protein: 2.6g
Carbohydrates: 2.8g

NUTTY MAPLE GRANOLA

Time: 30 minutes

Servings: 10

Ingredients:

8 cups rolled oats
1 cup coconut chips
½ cup almond slices
½ cup chopped pecans
½ cup walnuts, chopped

¼ cup virgin coconut oil, melted
½ cup maple syrup
1 pinch salt
1 teaspoon vanilla extract

Directions:

Combine the oats, coconut chips, almond slices, pecans and walnuts in a bowl.
Mix the coconut oil, maple syrup, salt and vanilla in a saucepan. Melt them together over low heat then pour over the oat mixture. Mix well.

Spread the mixture in a baking tray lined with parchment paper and bake in the preheated oven at 350F
   for 15 minutes or until golden brown and crisp.
Serve the granola chilled.

Nutritional information per serving

Calories: 374
Fat: 12.1g

Protein: 11g
Carbohydrates: 57.6g

BELL PEPPER GOAT CHEESE FRITTATA

Time: 35 minutes

Servings: 6

Ingredients:

4 eggs, beaten
½ teaspoon dried oregano
4 oz. goat cheese, crumbled
Salt and pepper to taste

2 tablespoons extra virgin olive oil
2 garlic cloves, minced
2 red bell peppers, cored and sliced
1 yellow bell pepper, cored and sliced

Directions:

Mix the eggs, oregano and goat cheese in a bowl. Adjust the taste with salt and pepper as needed.
Heat the oil in a skillet or frying pan. Add the garlic and bell peppers and cook for 2 minutes.
Pour the eggs over the peppers and cook on low heat for 8-10 minutes until set.
Serve the frittata warm and fresh.

Nutritional information per serving

Calories: 188
Fat: 14.5g

Protein: 10.1g
Carbohydrates: 4.7g

POMEGRANATE BERRY SMOOTHIE

Time: 10 minutes

Servings: 4

Ingredients:

2 cups mixed berries
1 cup pomegranate juice
1 cup coconut milk

2 tablespoons raw honey
1 tablespoon hemp seeds

Directions:

Combine all the ingredients in a blender and pulse until smooth.
Pour the smoothie into serving glasses and serve the smoothie fresh.

Nutritional information per serving

Calories: 258
Fat: 15.4g

Protein: 2.5g
Carbohydrates: 29.8g

Greek Omelet

Time: 25 minutes   Servings: 6

Ingredients:

4 eggs, beaten
½ cup crumbled feta cheese
2 green onions, chopped
1 tablespoon chopped parsley
½ teaspoon dried oregano

¼ teaspoon dried basil
Salt and pepper to taste
3 tablespoons extra virgin olive oil
1 tomato, peeled and diced
1 red bell pepper, cored and diced

Directions:

Combine the eggs, feta cheese, green onions, parsley, oregano and basil in a bowl. Add salt and pepper as needed.
Heat the oil in a frying pan then add the tomato and bell pepper. Cook for 2 minutes.
Pour the egg mixture over the tomatoes and lower the heat. Cook for 8-10 minutes until set.
Serve the omelet warm and fresh.

Nutritional information per serving

Calories: 145   Protein: 5.9g
Fat: 12.7g   Carbohydrates: 2.8g

Cinnamon Sweet Potato Pancakes

Time: 20 minutes   Servings: 4

Ingredients:

2 large sweet potatoes, cooked until tender, peeled and pureed
4 eggs   ¼ teaspoon ground ginger
¼ cup ground almonds   1 pinch salt
½ teaspoon cinnamon powder

Directions:

Combine all the ingredients in a bowl and mix well.
Heat a non-stick pan over medium pan.
Drop spoonfuls of batter on the hot pan and fry on each side until golden brown and set.
Serve the pancakes warm and fresh.

Nutritional information per serving

Calories: 146   Protein: 6.8g
Fat: 7.3g   Carbohydrates: 7.7g

Onion Turmeric Omelet

Time: 25 minutes

Servings: 4

Ingredients:

4 eggs, beaten
½ teaspoon turmeric powder
¼ teaspoon chili powder
½ teaspoon mustard seeds

2 green onions, chopped
Salt and pepper to taste
3 tablespoons extra virgin olive oil

Directions:

Combine the eggs, turmeric, chili powder, mustard seeds and onions in a bowl. Season with salt and pepper.

Heat the oil in a skillet or frying pan then pour in the omelet. Cook on each side until golden brown.

Serve the omelet warm and fresh.

Nutritional information per serving

Calories: 159
Fat: 15.1g

Protein: 5.8g
Carbohydrates: 1.3g

Poached Eggs in Avocados

Time: 15 minutes

Servings: 2

Ingredients:

2 cups water
½ teaspoon white wine vinegar
½ teaspoon salt

2 eggs
1 tablespoon lemon juice
1 avocado, halved

Directions:

Combine the water, vinegar and salt in a saucepan and bring to a boil.

Crack open the eggs and drop them in the boiling water. Cook for 1 minute at maximum just until the eggs are set on the outside, but still soft on the inside.

Drizzle the lemon juice over the avocado halves.

Drain the eggs and place one into each avocado half.

Serve right away.

Nutritional information per serving

Calories: 270
Fat: 24g

Protein: 7.5g
Carbohydrates: 9.2g

GREEK YOGURT PARFAITS

Time: 15 minutes

Servings: 4

Ingredients:

1 cup cooked quinoa
2 tablespoons raw honey

1 cup fresh blueberries
1½ cups plain Greek yogurt

Directions:

Mix the quinoa with honey.
Layer the quinoa, blueberries and yogurt into 4 small serving glasses.
Serve the parfaits fresh and chilled.

Nutritional information per serving

Calories: 292
Fat: 8g

Protein: 9.7g
Carbohydrates: 46.8g

QUINOA CRUSTED QUICHE

Time: 1 hour

Servings: 8

Ingredients:

Crust:

2 cups cooked quinoa
1 egg
¼ cup almond flour
¼ teaspoon salt

1 shallot, sliced
6 oz. baby spinach, shredded
6 eggs, beaten
½ cup buttermilk
2 oz. feta cheese, crumbled
Salt and pepper to taste

Filling:

2 tablespoons extra virgin olive oil

Directions:

For the crust, combine quinoa with the egg, flour and salt in a bowl and mix well.
Transfer the mixture in a quiche pan and press it well on the bottom and sides of the pan.
For the filling, heat the oil in a skillet and add the shallot. Cook for 1 minute then stir in the spinach. Cook for a few additional minutes then remove from heat and allow to cool down.
Add the rest of the ingredients then season with salt and pepper.
Pour the mixture into the quinoa crust and bake in the preheated oven at 350F for 30-35 minutes or until the center looks set and the edges turn golden brown.

Nutritional information per serving

Calories: 278
Fat: 12.1g

Protein: 13.2g
Carbohydrates: 29.6g

OATMEAL WITH BERRY COMPOTE

Time: 30 minutes   Servings: 4

Ingredients:

1 cup rolled oats   1 cup water
¼ cup dried cranberries   1 pinch salt
2 tablespoons raw honey   1 cup mixed berries
1 cup coconut milk   ½ cup fresh orange juice

Directions:

Combine the oats, cranberries, honey, coconut milk, water and a pinch of salt in a saucepan.
Cook just until softened, about 10-15 minutes.
For the compote, combine the berries with the orange juice in a saucepan and cook just 5 minutes to soften them up.
Spoon the cooked oatmeal in serving bowls then top with berry compote.
Serve the dish warm or chilled.

Nutritional information per serving

Calories: 285   Protein: 4.5g
Fat: 15.8g   Carbohydrates: 33.9g

BUTTON MUSHROOM FRITTATA

Time: 40 minutes   Servings: 6

Ingredients:

2 tablespoons extra virgin olive oil   4 eggs, beaten
2 garlic cloves, minced   2 tablespoons chopped parsley
1 pound button mushrooms   Salt and pepper to taste

Directions:

Heat the oil in a frying pan or skillet. Add the garlic and mushrooms and cook for a few minutes until softened.
In a bowl, mix the eggs and parsley and add salt and pepper to taste.
Pour the mixture over the mushrooms then lower the heat and cook the frittata on each side for 5-10 minutes until set and golden brown.
Serve the frittata warm and fresh.

Nutritional information per serving

Calories: 100   Protein: 6.2g
Fat: 7.8g   Carbohydrates: 3.1g

QUICK BANANA PANCAKES

Time: 15 minutes

Servings: 6

Ingredients:

4 eggs
2 large bananas, mashed

8 tablespoons almond flour
1 pinch salt

Directions:

Mix the eggs with bananas until creamy.
Stir in the almond flour and salt and mix well.
Heat a non-stick pan over medium flame then drop spoonfuls of batter on the hot pan.
Cook on each side for a few minutes until golden brown.
Serve the pancakes warm and fresh.

Nutritional information per serving

Calories: 296
Fat: 21.7g

Protein: 12.2g
Carbohydrates: 18.6g

SUMMER VEGETABLE FRITTATA

Time: 40 minutes

Servings: 6

Ingredients:

2 tablespoons extra virgin olive oil
2 garlic cloves, chopped
1 red bell pepper, cored and sliced
1 small zucchini, sliced
1 shallot, sliced

1 cup cherry tomatoes, halved
4 eggs, beaten
1 pinch chili flakes
Salt and pepper to taste

Directions:

Heat the oil in a frying pan or skillet. Add the garlic and vegetables and cook for 5-7 minutes until softened.
Mix the eggs, chili flakes, salt and pepper in a bowl.
Pour this mixture over the vegetables then lower the heat and cook on each side for 5 minutes until set and golden.
Serve the frittata warm and fresh.

Nutritional information per serving

Calories: 99
Fat: 7.8g

Protein: 4.5g
Carbohydrates: 3.9g

ALMOND BUTTER SMOOTHIE BOWLS

Time: 20 minutes   Servings: 4

Ingredients:

1 cup fresh strawberries
½ cup plain yogurt
2 tablespoons almond butter
1 cup coconut milk
2 tablespoons raw honey

½ cup fresh blueberries
½ cup cornflakes
2 tablespoons sunflower seeds
2 tablespoons flax seeds

Directions:

Combine the strawberries, yogurt, almond butter, coconut milk and honey in a blender and pulse until smooth.

Pour the smoothie into 2 serving bowls and top each bowl with blueberries, cornflakes, sunflower seeds and flax seeds.

Serve the bowls fresh.

Nutritional information per serving

Calories: 304   Protein: 6.4g
Fat: 21.2g   Carbohydrates: 25.2g

AVOCADO STRAWBERRY SMOOTHIE

Time: 10 minutes   Servings: 4

Ingredients:

1 avocado, peeled and pitted
1 cup fresh strawberries
¼ cup plain yogurt

1 cup coconut milk
1 tablespoon raw honey

Directions:

Combine all the ingredients in a blender.

Pulse until smooth and creamy then pour into serving glasses and serve as fresh as possible as it tends to oxidize quickly.

Nutritional information per serving

Calories: 279   Protein: 3.5g
Fat: 24.4g   Carbohydrates: 15.8g

Coconut Quinoa Pudding

Time: 30 minutes

Servings: 6

Ingredients:

½ cup quinoa, rinsed
1 cup coconut flakes
2 tablespoons chia seeds

1 cup coconut milk
½ cup water
2 tablespoons raw honey

Directions:

Combine all the ingredients in a saucepan.
Cook on low heat for 20 minutes or until most of the liquid has been absorbed.
Serve the pudding warm or chilled.

Nutritional information per serving

Calories: 265
Fat: 18.1g

Protein: 5.5g
Carbohydrates: 22.6g

Pomegranate Millet Salad

Time: 25 minutes

Servings: 6

Ingredients:

1 cup millet
½ cup coconut milk
1½ cups water
¼ teaspoon dried mint
2 tablespoons raw honey

1 cup pomegranate seeds
¼ cup pistachios, toasted
2 tablespoons extra virgin olive oil
2 tablespoons tahini paste

Directions:

Combine the millet, coconut milk, water, mint and honey in a saucepan.
Cook for 15-20 minutes until all the liquid has been absorbed.
Fluff up the millet mix and transfer it in a salad bowl.
Stir in the pomegranate seeds and pistachios then drizzle with olive oil and tahini paste.
Mix well and serve the salad fresh.

Nutritional information per serving

Calories: 276
Fat: 14.7g

Protein: 5.5g
Carbohydrates: 32.9g

CREAMY COCONUT QUINOA PUDDING

Time: 25 minutes   Servings: 4

Ingredients:

⅔ cup quinoa, rinsed   ½ cup water
½ cup shredded coconut   2 tablespoons raw honey
1½ cups coconut milk   1 pinch salt

Directions:

Combine the quinoa, coconut, coconut milk, water, honey and salt in a saucepan.
Cook over low heat for 15-20 minutes or until the liquid has been absorbed and the pudding is creamy
    and thickened.
Serve the pudding chilled.

Nutritional information per serving

Calories: 379   Protein: 6.4g
Fat: 26.5g   Carbohydrates: 33.3g

VEGETABLES IN TOMATO SAUCE

Time: 30 minutes   Servings: 4

Ingredients:

2 tablespoons extra virgin olive oil   1 cup diced tomatoes
1 zucchini, cubed   ½ cup water
1 small eggplant, peeled and cubed   Salt and pepper to taste
1 red bell pepper, cored and sliced   4 eggs
2 garlic cloves, minced   2 tablespoons chopped parsley
¼ teaspoon smoked paprika

Directions:

Heat the oil in a skillet or frying pan then add the zucchini, eggplant, bell pepper, garlic and paprika.
Cook for 2 minutes then stir in the tomatoes, water, salt and pepper.
Cook for 10 minutes on low heat.
Crack open the eggs and drop them in the hot liquid.
Sprinkle with chopped parsley and cook just for a few additional minutes until the eggs are set.
Serve the veggies and eggs right away.

Nutritional information per serving

Calories: 180   Protein: 8.1g
Fat: 11.9g   Carbohydrates: 13.0g

Butternut Squash Oatmeal

Time: 30 minutes

Servings: 4

Ingredients:

2 tablespoons extra virgin olive oil
1 cup butternut squash cubes
1 cup rolled oats
1 cup coconut milk
½ cup water

2 tablespoons raw honey
1 cinnamon stick
1 star anise
1 whole clove
1 pinch salt

Directions:

Heat the oil in a saucepan and add the butternut squash cubes. Cook for 2 minutes until golden then add the rest of the ingredients.
Cover the pot and cook on low heat for 15 minutes.
Serve the oatmeal chilled.

Nutritional information per serving

Calories: 322
Fat: 22.8g

Protein: 4.5g
Carbohydrates: 29.3g

Banana Peach Smoothie

Time: 10 minutes

Servings: 4

Ingredients:

1 banana
2 peaches, pitted and sliced
1 cup pineapple juice

1 cup coconut water
2 tablespoons chia seeds
1 tablespoon raw honey

Directions:

Combine all the ingredients in a blender.
Pulse until smooth and creamy.
Pour the smoothie into glasses and serve the smoothie fresh.

Nutritional information per serving

Calories: 184
Fat: 5.2g

Protein: 4.6g
Carbohydrates: 31.3g

Lunch Recipes

Sweet Potato Casserole

Time: 40 minutes   Servings: 8

Ingredients:

2 pounds sweet potatoes, peeled and cubed
1 shallot, chopped
1 jalapeño, chopped
4 garlic cloves, minced

1 yellow bell pepper, cored and diced
2 tablespoons chopped cilantro
Salt and pepper to taste
6 eggs, beaten

Directions:

Combine all the ingredients in a deep dish baking pan.
Season with salt and pepper and cook in the preheated oven at 350F for 25-30 minutes or until golden brown.
Serve the casserole warm or chilled.

Nutritional information per serving

Calories: 189
Fat: 3.5g

Protein: 6.2g
Carbohydrates: 33.5g

Sausage Broccoli Bake

Time: 40 minutes   Servings: 8

Ingredients:

2 tablespoons extra virgin olive oil
8 oz. mushrooms, sliced
10 oz. chicken sausages, skin removed and crumbled
1 pound broccoli, cut into florets
6 eggs, beaten

½ cup coconut milk
Salt and pepper to taste
½ teaspoon dried oregano
½ teaspoon dried basil
8 oz. mozzarella cheese, shredded

Directions:

Heat the oil in a frying pan or skillet and add the mushrooms. Cook for 10 minutes, stirring often, then remove from heat and transfer in a deep dish baking pan.
Add the sausages and the remaining ingredients and cook in the preheated oven at 350F for 30 minutes.
Serve the bake warm and fresh.

Nutritional information per serving

Calories: 266

Fat: 19.4g

Protein: 18.1g

Carbohydrates: 5.5g

Mediterranean Vegetable Fry Up

Time: 40 minutes

Servings: 6

Ingredients:

3 tablespoons extra virgin olive oil
2 potatoes, peeled and diced
1 red bell pepper, cored and sliced
1 yellow bell pepper, cored and sliced
1 shallot, sliced
1 zucchini, sliced

1 eggplant, peeled and sliced
½ teaspoon dried oregano
½ teaspoon dried basil
1 pinch garlic powder
Salt and pepper to taste
1 tablespoon lemon juice

Directions:

Heat the oil in a skillet or frying pan. Add the rest of the ingredients and cook for about 15 minutes over medium heat, stirring often.

Serve the fry up warm and fresh.

Nutritional information per serving

Calories: 148

Fat: 7.4g

Protein: 2.8g

Carbohydrates: 19.6g

Mediterranean Tuna Salad

Time: 20 minutes

Servings: 6

Ingredients:

1 can water packed tuna, drained
4 roasted bell peppers, chopped
¼ cup pitted black olives
4 artichoke hearts, drained and chopped
½ teaspoon dried basil

½ teaspoon dried oregano
2 tablespoons chopped parsley
2 cups arugula leaves
2 tablespoons balsamic vinegar
Salt and pepper to taste

Directions:

Combine the tuna, peppers, black olives, artichoke hearts, herbs, parsley and arugula in a bowl.

Drizzle with vinegar and season with salt and pepper.

Serve the salad fresh.

Nutritional information per serving

Calories: 103

Fat: 1.1g

Protein: 10.8g

Carbohydrates: 12.2g

MINESTRONE SOUP

Time: 45 minutes

Servings: 8

Ingredients:

2 tablespoons extra virgin olive oil
1 shallot, chopped
1 red bell pepper, cored and diced
2 carrots, diced
1 parsnip, diced
1 celery stalk, sliced
1 zucchini, cubed
2 cups green beans, chopped

½ cup green peas
2 cups baby spinach
1 cup diced tomatoes
4 cups water
2 cups vegetable stock
½ teaspoon dried oregano
½ teaspoon dried basil
Salt and pepper to taste

Directions:

Combine the olive oil and the vegetables in a soup pot.
Add the water, stock and herbs, as well as salt and pepper and cook on medium heat for 20-25 minutes.
Serve the soup warm and fresh, although it tastes just as good chilled.

Nutritional information per serving

Calories: 82
Fat: 3.8g

Protein: 2.3g
Carbohydrates: 11.2g

TOMATO SALAD WITH PITA CROUTONS

Time: 20 minutes

Servings: 4

Ingredients:

Croutons:

4 pita breads, sliced
3 tablespoons extra virgin olive oil
1 teaspoon dried oregano
½ teaspoon chili powder
½ teaspoon salt

Salad:

4 tomatoes, cubed
1 cucumber, sliced
1 shallot, sliced
2 tablespoons chopped cilantro
Salt and pepper to taste

Directions:

For the croutons, place the pita bread slices on a baking tray. Drizzle with olive oil and sprinkle with oregano, chili powder and salt.
Bake in the preheated oven at 350F for 10 minutes.
For the salad, combine the tomatoes, cucumber, shallot and cilantro in a bowl. Add salt and pepper to taste.
Serve the salad fresh, topped with croutons.

Nutritional information per serving

Calories: 293
Fat: 11.7g

Protein: 7.2g
Carbohydrates: 41.8g

Zucchini Rosemary Pita Bread Pizza

Time: 20 minutes

Servings: 2

Ingredients:

2 pita breads
½ cup sour cream
1 tablespoon chopped cilantro
1 tablespoon chopped parsley

1 teaspoon dried rosemary
1 zucchini, sliced
Salt and pepper to taste

Directions:

Place the pita breads on a baking tray lined with baking paper.
Spread sour cream on both breads and top with cilantro, parsley and rosemary.
Arrange the zucchini on top and season with salt and pepper.
Cook in the preheated oven at 350F for 8-10 minutes.
Serve the pizza warm.

Nutritional information per serving

Calories: 307
Fat: 13.1g

Protein: 8.6g
Carbohydrates: 39.7g

Chunky Vegetable Salad

Time: 30 minutes

Servings: 4

Ingredients:

4 tomatoes, cubed
1 cup cooked chickpeas, drained
1 jalapeño pepper, chopped
1 red bell pepper, cored and diced
1 celery stalk, sliced
1 cucumber, sliced

2 tablespoons olive oil
1 tablespoon balsamic vinegar
1 tablespoon chopped parsley
1 tablespoon chopped cilantro
Salt and pepper to taste

Directions:

Combine all the ingredients in a salad bowl.
Add salt and pepper to taste and serve the salad warm and fresh.

Nutritional information per serving

Calories: 288
Fat: 10.5g

Protein: 11.6g
Carbohydrates: 40.1g

Chicken Celery Salad

Time: 25 minutes

Servings: 4

Ingredients:

2 chicken breasts, cubed
2 celery stalks, sliced
1 cucumber, sliced
2 tablespoons chopped parsley

¼ cup Greek style yogurt
Salt and pepper to taste
1 tablespoon lemon juice

Directions:

Combine all the ingredients in a bowl.
Season with salt and pepper and serve the salad fresh.

Nutritional information per serving

Calories: 167
Fat: 6.3g

Protein: 20.9g
Carbohydrates: 3.2g

Mediterranean Barley Salad

Time: 1 hour

Servings: 6

Ingredients:

1 cup pearl barley, rinsed
2 cups water
2 chicken breasts, cooked and diced
1 celery stalk, sliced
1 cucumber, sliced
4 roasted red bell peppers, chopped

2 tablespoons chopped parsley
2 cups cherry tomatoes, halved
1 red onion, sliced
Salt and pepper to taste
4 oz. feta cheese, crumbled

Directions:

Combine the pearl barley and water in a saucepan. Cook on low heat for 30 minutes until softened.
Transfer the pearl barley in a bowl then stir in the rest of the ingredients. Season with salt and pepper.
Serve the salad fresh.

Nutritional information per serving

Calories: 299
Fat: 8.1g

Protein: 21.3g
Carbohydrates: 36.7g

SPINACH LENTIL STEW

Time: 40 minutes   Servings: 8

Ingredients:

3 tablespoons extra virgin olive oil
2 garlic cloves, chopped
2 shallots, sliced
1 red bell pepper, cored and diced
1 carrot, diced
1 celery stalk, diced
½ teaspoon turmeric powder
¼ teaspoon chili powder

½ teaspoon garam masala
1 cup diced tomatoes
1 cup green lentils, rinsed
2 cups water
1 bay leaf
Salt and pepper to taste
2 cups baby spinach

Directions:

Heat the oil in a saucepan. Add the garlic and shallots and cook for 2 minutes until softened.
Add the rest of the ingredients, except the spinach, and season with salt and pepper.
Cook on low heat for 20 minutes until creamy and cooked through.
Add the spinach and cook for 5 additional minutes.
Serve the stew warm and fresh.

Nutritional information per serving

Calories: 147   Protein: 7.0g
Fat: 5.6g   Carbohydrates: 18.1g

SPINACH GRAPEFRUIT SALAD

Time: 30 minutes   Servings: 4

Ingredients:

4 cups baby spinach
2 grapefruits, cut into segments
1 red onion, sliced
¼ cup hazelnuts, chopped

½ cup plain yogurt
2 tablespoons lemon juice
2 tablespoons extra virgin olive oil
Salt and pepper to taste

Directions:

Combine the baby spinach, grapefruits, onion and hazelnuts in a bowl.
Combine the yogurt, lemon juice, olive oil, salt and pepper in a glass jar. Shake until creamy.
Drizzle the dressing over the salad and serve it fresh.

Nutritional information per serving

Calories: 151   Protein: 4.1g
Fat: 10.5g   Carbohydrates: 11.9g

Herbed Quinoa Salad

Time: 30 minutes

Servings: 6

Ingredients:

1 cup quinoa, rinsed
2½ cups water
1 cup chopped parsley
½ cup chopped cilantro
2 oranges, cut into segments

½ teaspoon dried basil
½ teaspoon dried oregano
2 tablespoons lemon juice
Salt and pepper to taste
2 tablespoons extra virgin olive oil

Directions:

Combine the quinoa and water, as well as a pinch of salt in a saucepan. Cook for 20-25 minutes until softened.

Transfer the quinoa in a salad bowl.

Add the rest of the ingredients and season with salt and pepper.

Serve the salad fresh.

Nutritional information per serving

Calories: 179
Fat: 6.6g

Protein: 5.0g
Carbohydrates: 26.3g

Zucchini Boats

Time: 45 minutes

Servings: 4

Ingredients:

2 zucchinis
1 pound ground chicken
1 teaspoon dried basil
1 teaspoon dried oregano
2 tablespoons chopped parsley

1 shallot, chopped
Salt and pepper to taste
1 cup tomato sauce
½ cup dry white wine
1 bay leaf

Directions:

Cut the zucchinis in half and carefully scoop out the flesh. Chop the zucchini flesh finely and place it in a bowl.

Add the ground chicken, basil, oregano, parsley and shallot and season with salt and pepper.

Spoon the mixture back into the zucchini boats.

Place the zucchini in a deep dish baking tray and pour in the tomato sauce and wine. Add the bay leaf as well as salt and pepper to taste.

Cook in the preheated oven at 350F for 15-20 minutes.

Serve the zucchini boats warm and fresh.

Nutritional information per serving

Calories: 275
Fat: 8.8g

Protein: 35.0g
Carbohydrates: 8.4g

Imam Bayaldi

Time: 45 minutes

Servings: 8

Ingredients:

2 eggplants
2 tablespoons extra virgin olive oil
2 garlic cloves, minced
1 shallot, chopped
2 tablespoons chopped parsley
1 pound ground beef
1 tablespoon lemon juice

½ teaspoon cumin powder
¼ teaspoon chili powder
Salt and pepper to taste
1 cup tomato sauce
1 cup vegetable stock
1 bay leaf
8 oz. shredded mozzarella cheese

Directions:

Cut the eggplants in half lengthwise and carefully remove the flesh, leaving the skins intact. Chop the flesh finely.

Heat the oil in a skillet and add the eggplants. Cook until softened then stir in the garlic, shallot, parsley, ground beef, lemon juice and spices, as well as salt and pepper.

Spoon the mixture into each eggplant skin.

Place the imam bayaldi in a deep dish baking tray. Pour in the sauce, stock and bay leaf and cook in the preheated oven at 350F for 25-30 minutes or until softened.

Garnish with cheese and serve the dish warm and fresh.

Nutritional information per serving

Calories: 263
Fat: 12.5g

Protein: 27.3g
Carbohydrates: 11.6g

Quinoa Berry Salad

Time: 30 minutes

Servings: 4

Ingredients:

¾ cup quinoa, rinsed
1 cup vegetable stock
1 cup water
2 cups arugula leaves
1 cup mixed berries
2 tablespoons chopped parsley
1 teaspoon dried mint

1 lemon, juiced
1 tablespoon poppy seeds
2 tablespoons extra virgin olive oil
Salt and pepper to taste

Directions:

Combine the quinoa, water and stock in a saucepan and cook over low heat for 15-20 minutes until softened.

Transfer the quinoa in a salad bowl and stir in the arugula leaves, berries, parsley and mint.

For the dressing, combine the lemon juice, poppy seeds, olive oil, salt and pepper in a jar. Cover the jar and shake well until creamy.

Drizzle the dressing over the salad and serve it fresh.

Nutritional information per serving

Calories: 198

Fat: 10.1g

Protein: 5.5g

Carbohydrates: 23.1g

GREEN ASPARAGUS SOUP

Time: 30 minutes

Servings: 6

Ingredients:

2 tablespoons extra virgin olive oil

1 shallot, chopped

2 garlic cloves, minced

1 jalapeño pepper, chopped

1 celery stalk, sliced

1 pound asparagus, trimmed and chopped

2 cups vegetable stock

2 cups water

1 tablespoon lemon juice

Salt and pepper to taste

Directions:

Heat the oil in a soup pot and stir in the shallot and garlic. Cook for 1 minute until softened then add the pepper, celery and asparagus.

Stir in the stock, water and lemon juice then add salt and pepper to taste.

Cook on low heat for 20 minutes.

When done, remove from heat and puree the soup with an immersion blender until creamy.

Serve the soup warm and fresh.

Nutritional information per serving

Calories: 62

Fat: 4.8g

Protein: 2.0g

Carbohydrates: 4.1g

BLACK BEAN QUINOA SALAD

Time: 30 minutes

Servings: 6

Ingredients:

1 cup quinoa, rinsed

2 cups water

1 red bell pepper, cored and sliced

1 yellow bell pepper, cored and sliced

1 can black beans, drained

½ cup canned corn, drained

1 red onion, sliced
2 tablespoons chopped cilantro

1 lemon, juiced
Salt and pepper to taste

Directions:

Combine the quinoa and water in a saucepan and cook over low heat for 15 minutes until the water is absorbed.

Transfer the cooked quinoa in a salad bowl.

Add the rest of the ingredients and season with salt and pepper as needed.

Serve the salad fresh.

Nutritional information per serving

Calories: 247
Fat: 2.4g

Protein: 12.0g
Carbohydrates: 45.8g

TAHINI ARUGULA CHICKEN SALAD

Time: 30 minutes

Servings: 4

Ingredients:

1 chicken breasts, cut into strips
1 tablespoon Cajun seasoning
Salt and pepper to taste
4 cups arugula

2 garlic cloves, minced
2 tablespoons tahini paste
1 lemon, juiced
2 tablespoons extra virgin olive oil

Directions:

Season the chicken with Cajun seasoning, salt and pepper.

Heat a grill pan over medium flame and place the chicken on the grill. Cook on each side for a few minutes until golden and the juices run out clean.

Place the arugula on a platter. Top with chicken.

For the dressing, mix the garlic, tahini paste, lemon juice and olive oil, as well as salt and pepper.

Drizzle the dressing over the salad and serve right away.

Nutritional information per serving

Calories: 183
Fat: 13.8g

Protein: 12.2g
Carbohydrates: 4.2g

QUINOA TABBOULEH

Time: 30 minutes

Servings: 6

Ingredients:

1 cup quinoa, rinsed
2 cups water

Salt and pepper to taste
2 cups cherry tomatoes, halved

1 cup chopped parsley
½ cup chopped cilantro
1 cucumber, sliced

1 red chili, chopped
1 lemon, juiced
2 tablespoons extra virgin olive oil

Directions:

Combine the quinoa, water, salt and pepper in a saucepan and cook on low heat for 15-20 minutes.
Remove from heat and transfer the quinoa in a salad bowl.
Add the rest of the ingredients and mix well.
Season with salt and pepper if needed and serve the tabbouleh fresh.

Nutritional information per serving

Calories: 170
Fat: 6.7g

Protein: 5.3g
Carbohydrates: 24.0g

GREEN AVOCADO SOUP

Time: 20 minutes

Servings: 4

Ingredients:

1 avocado, peeled and sliced
½ cup fresh coriander
2 garlic cloves
¼ teaspoon grated ginger
1 zucchini, sliced

1 cup broccoli florets
2 cups water
1 tablespoon lemon juice
2 kale leaves
Salt and pepper to taste

Directions:

Combine all the ingredients in a blender and pulse until smooth and creamy.
Add salt and pepper and serve the soup warm and fresh.

Nutritional information per serving

Calories: 139
Fat: 10.0g

Protein: 3.4g
Carbohydrates: 11.7g

CREAMY RED LENTIL CARROT SOUP

Time: 35 minutes

Servings: 6

Ingredients:

3 tablespoons extra virgin olive oil
1 shallot, chopped
1 jalapeño pepper, chopped
2 garlic cloves, minced
2 carrots, sliced
1 cup red lentils, rinsed

2 cups water
2 cups vegetable stock
1 tablespoon lemon juice
½ teaspoon cumin powder
¼ teaspoon chili powder
Salt and pepper to taste

Directions:

Heat the oil in a soup pot and stir in the shallot, jalapeño and garlic. Cook for a few seconds only then add the rest of the ingredients.

Season with salt and pepper and cook on low heat for 20 minutes.

When done, remove from heat and puree the soup with an immersion blender.

Serve the soup warm and fresh.

Nutritional information per serving

Calories: 188

Fat: 7.5g

Protein: 8.8g

Carbohydrates: 22.5g

Tuna Stuffed Sweet Potatoes

Time: 30 minutes

Servings: 2

Ingredients:

2 sweet potatoes

1 can water packed tuna, drained

½ cup cottage cheese

2 tablespoons chopped parsley

½ jalapeño, chopped

1 green onion, chopped

Salt and pepper to taste

Directions:

Wrap the sweet potatoes in aluminum foil and cook in the preheated oven at 350F for 20 minutes.

Mix the tuna, cheese, parsley, jalapeño, onion, salt and pepper in a bowl.

Remove from the oven and cut each potato in half. Stuff the potatoes with the tuna mixture and cook for 10 additional minutes.

Serve the sweet potatoes warm.

Nutritional information per serving

Calories: 327

Fat: 2.1g

Protein: 31g

Carbohydrates: 44.7g

Asian Chicken Salad

Time: 30 minutes

Servings: 6

Ingredients:

2 chicken breasts, cooked and diced

2 cups arugula

1 red onion, sliced

1 green onion, sliced

2 tablespoons chopped parsley

1 tablespoon fish sauce

1 lime, juiced

1 teaspoon honey

1 tablespoon soy sauce

Directions:

Combine the chicken, arugula, red onion, green onion and parsley in a salad bowl.

For the dressing, mix the fish sauce, lime juice, honey and soy sauce in a bowl. Mix well then drizzle the dressing over the salad.

Serve the salad fresh.

Nutritional information per serving

Calories: 125

Fat: 3.5g

Protein: 14.3g

Carbohydrates: 3.5g

COBB SALAD WITH BUTTERMILK DRESSING

Time: 30 minutes

Servings: 6

Ingredients:

1 head lettuce, shredded
1 avocado, peeled and sliced
1 cup cherry tomatoes, halved
1 chicken breast, cooked and diced
2 hard-boiled eggs, sliced

½ cup buttermilk
2 tablespoons lemon juice
2 tablespoons extra virgin olive oil
Salt and pepper to taste

Directions:

Combine the lettuce, avocado, tomatoes, chicken and eggs in a salad bowl.

For the dressing, mix the buttermilk, lemon juice, olive oil, salt and pepper in a glass jar. Seal the jar and shake it to mix the dressing well.

Drizzle the dressing over the salad and mix gently.

Serve the salad fresh.

Nutritional information per serving

Calories: 199

Fat: 14.1g

Protein: 12.9g

Carbohydrates: 6.9g

PRAWN SWEET CORN SALAD

Time: 30 minutes

Servings: 6

Ingredients:

1 pound fresh prawns, peeled and deveined
1 head lettuce, shredded
2 hard-boiled eggs, cubed
1 cup sweet corn, drained
1 cucumber, sliced

1 tablespoon mustard
2 tablespoons lemon juice
3 tablespoons extra virgin olive oil
Salt and pepper to taste

Directions:

Cook the prawns on a grill pan until golden on each side. Place aside.

Combine the lettuce, eggs, corn and cucumber in a salad bowl. Place the prawns on top.

For the dressing, mix the mustard, lemon juice and oil in a glass jar. Add salt and pepper and seal the jar. Shake it well then drizzle the dressing over the salad.

Serve the salad fresh.

Nutritional information per serving

Calories: 216

Fat: 10.7g

Protein: 20.8g

Carbohydrates: 10.4g

Tuna Rice Salad

Time: 35 minutes

Servings: 6

Ingredients:

1 cup wild rice

2 cups water

½ cup coconut milk

1 bay leaf

1 can water packed tuna, drained

2 green onions, sliced

2 red bell peppers, cored and sliced

1 jalapeño pepper, chopped

½ cup green olives, sliced

2 tablespoons chopped parsley

2 tablespoons lemon juice

Salt and pepper to taste

Directions:

Combine the rice, water, coconut milk and bay leaf in a saucepan. Cook on low heat until the rice has absorbed the liquid.

Transfer the rice in a salad bowl.

Add the rest of the ingredients and season with salt and pepper.

Mix well and serve the salad fresh.

Nutritional information per serving

Calories: 202

Fat: 5.9g

Protein: 14.2g

Carbohydrates: 24.3g

White Bean Tuna Salad

Time: 30 minutes

Servings: 6

Ingredients:

2 cans white beans, drained

1 can water packed tuna, drained

2 green onions, sliced

1 red chili, chopped

1 red onion, sliced

½ cup sweet corn, drained

1 teaspoon capers, drained and chopped

2 tablespoons extra virgin olive oil

2 tablespoons lemon juice
Salt and pepper to taste

½ teaspoon dried oregano

Directions:

Combine the beans, tuna, green onions, chili, onion, corn, capers, oil and lemon juice in a salad bowl.
Add the rest of the ingredients and mix well.
Serve the salad fresh.

Nutritional information per serving

Calories: 318
Fat: 5.8g

Protein: 23.5g
Carbohydrates: 45.5g

CREAMY GARLIC ZUCCHINI SOUP

Time: 35 minutes

Servings: 6

Ingredients:

2 tablespoons extra virgin olive oil
4 garlic cloves, chopped
1 shallot, chopped
3 zucchinis, cubed
2 potatoes, peeled and cubed

2 cups water
2 cups vegetable stock
Salt and pepper to taste
Plain yogurt for serving

Directions:

Heat the oil in a soup pot and add the garlic and shallot. Cook for a few seconds then add the rest of the ingredients.
Season with salt and pepper and cook on low heat for 15 minutes.
When done, puree the soup with an immersion blender.
Pour the soup into serving bowls and top with plain yogurt. Serve right away.

Nutritional information per serving

Calories: 111
Fat: 5.0g

Protein: 2.7g
Carbohydrates: 15.7g

INDIAN CHICKPEA SOUP

Time: 35 minutes

Servings: 6

Ingredients:

3 tablespoons extra virgin olive oil
1 shallot, chopped
2 garlic cloves, minced
½ teaspoon grated ginger
½ teaspoon turmeric powder

1 teaspoon garam masala
1 can chickpeas, drained
2 carrots, diced
1 celery stalk, diced
1 red bell pepper, cored and diced

2 cups water
2 cups vegetable stock

Salt and pepper to taste
2 cups baby spinach

Directions:

Heat the oil in a soup pot and stir in the shallot, garlic and spices. Cook for a few seconds until fragrant then add the chickpeas, carrots, celery, bell pepper, water and stock, as well as salt and pepper.
Cook on low heat for 15-20 minutes then add the spinach and cook for another 5 minutes.
Serve the soup warm and fresh.

Nutritional information per serving

Calories: 204
Fat: 9.2g

Protein: 7.4g
Carbohydrates: 25.0g

Roasted Bell Pepper Chickpea Salad

Time: 20 minutes

Servings: 4

Ingredients:

1 cup chickpeas, drained
4 roasted red bell peppers, chopped
2 garlic cloves, minced
1 red onion, sliced
½ teaspoon dried mint

2 tablespoons chopped parsley
2 green onions, chopped
2 tablespoons lemon juice
2 tablespoons extra virgin olive oil
Salt and pepper to taste

Directions:

Combine the chickpeas with the rest of the ingredients and season with salt and pepper.
Mix the salad well and serve it fresh.

Nutritional information per serving

Calories: 285
Fat: 10.1g

Protein: 11.3g
Carbohydrates: 40.2g

Avocado Dressed Salad

Time: 25 minutes

Servings: 4

Ingredients:

1 avocado, peeled
2 garlic cloves
2 tablespoons lemon juice
2 tablespoons extra virgin olive oil

½ teaspoon hot sauce
Salt and pepper to taste
2 cups chicken breasts, cooked and diced
1 cucumber, diced

Directions:

Combine the avocado, garlic, lemon juice, olive oil, hot sauce, salt and pepper in a blender. Pulse until smooth and creamy.

Combine the chicken and cucumber in a bowl. Add the dressing and mix gently.

Serve the salad fresh.

Nutritional information per serving

Calories: 311

Fat: 22.1g

Protein: 21.8g

Carbohydrates: 7.7g

Moroccan Chickpea Soup

Time: 35 minutes

Servings: 6

Ingredients:

1 can chickpeas, drained
2 tablespoons extra virgin olive oil
1 shallot, chopped
2 garlic cloves, minced
1 red bell pepper, cored and diced
1 yellow bell pepper, cored and diced
1 celery stalk, sliced
½ teaspoon cumin powder
½ teaspoon garam masala

¼ teaspoon chili powder
1 can diced tomatoes
2 cups water
3 cups vegetable stock
2 tablespoons lemon juice
2 tablespoons chopped parsley
½ teaspoon dried thyme
Salt and pepper to taste

Directions:

Combine the chickpeas, olive oil, shallot and the rest of the ingredients in a soup pot.

Add salt and pepper to taste and cook on low heat for 25 minutes.

Serve the soup warm and fresh.

Nutritional information per serving

Calories: 184

Fat: 7g

Protein: 7.4g

Carbohydrates: 24.4g

Green Pea Hummus

Time: 15 minutes

Servings: 4

Ingredients:

1½ cups green peas
1 cup chickpeas, drained
4 garlic cloves
1 pinch chili flakes

2 tablespoons lemon juice
3 tablespoons extra virgin olive oil
Salt and pepper to taste

Directions:

Pour 1 cup of water in a pot and add the green peas. Cook on low heat for 5 minutes then drain and place in a food processor.

Add the rest of the ingredients and season with salt and pepper.

Pulse until the hummus is creamy.

Serve it chilled.

Nutritional information per serving

Calories: 322

Fat: 13.8g

Protein: 12.9g

Carbohydrates: 39.3g

ARTICHOKE DIP

Time: 15 minutes

Servings: 4

Ingredients:

1 jar artichoke hearts, drained

½ teaspoon dried mint

1 cup cooked green lentils

3 tablespoons extra virgin olive oil

2 tablespoons lemon juice

¼ teaspoon cumin powder

1 pinch chili flakes

Salt and pepper to taste

Directions:

Combine the artichoke hearts and the rest of the ingredients in a food processor.

Add salt and pepper to taste and pulse until smooth and creamy.

Serve the dip fresh.

Nutritional information per serving

Calories: 292

Fat: 14.1g

Protein: 13.5g

Carbohydrates: 29.1g

GREEN GAZPACHO

Time: 20 minutes

Servings: 4

Ingredients:

1 celery stalk, sliced

1 cucumber, sliced

2 garlic cloves

2 cups baby spinach

1 jalapeño

1 avocado, pitted

½ cup cilantro leaves

¼ cup chopped parsley

2 tablespoons sunflower seeds

2 tablespoons lemon juice

2 tablespoons extra virgin olive oil

½ teaspoon sumac seasoning

2 cups water

Salt and pepper to taste

Directions:

Combine all the ingredients in a blender.

Add salt and pepper to taste and pulse until smooth and creamy.

Pour the gazpacho into serving bowls and serve it fresh.

Nutritional information per serving

Calories: 193

Fat: 17.8g

Protein: 2.6g

Carbohydrates: 9.2g

BERRILICIOUS SPINACH SALAD

Time: 20 minutes

Servings: 2

Ingredients:

3 cups baby spinach

1 cup strawberries, halved

1 red onion, sliced

1 can water packed tuna, drained

1 tablespoon white wine vinegar

1 tablespoon lemon juice

1 teaspoon mustard

2 tablespoons extra virgin olive oil

Salt and pepper to taste

Directions:

Combine the spinach, strawberries, red onion and tuna in a salad bowl.

For the dressing, mix the vinegar, lemon juice, mustard and olive oil in a bowl. Add salt and pepper to taste and mix well.

Drizzle the dressing over the salad and serve it fresh.

Nutritional information per serving

Calories: 232

Fat: 15.5g

Protein: 12.3g

Carbohydrates: 13.1g

AVOCADO SPINACH SALAD

Time: 20 minutes

Servings: 4

Ingredients:

3 cups baby spinach

1 avocado, peeled and cubed

1 cup cherry tomatoes, halved

½ cup sweet corn, drained

2 tablespoons pine nuts

1 teaspoon Dijon mustard

2 tablespoons extra virgin olive oil

2 tablespoons white wine vinegar

Salt and pepper to taste

Directions:

Combine the spinach, avocado, tomatoes, corn and pine nuts in a salad bowl.

For the dressing, mix the mustard, oil and vinegar in a bowl. Mix well, adding salt and pepper to taste. Drizzle the dressing over the salad.
Serve the salad fresh.

Nutritional information per serving

Calories: 223
Fat: 20.1g

Protein: 3.1g
Carbohydrates: 11.3g

SPINACH PINEAPPLE SALAD

Time: 20 minutes

Servings: 2

Ingredients:

2 cups baby spinach
1 fresh pineapple, peeled, cored and sliced
¼ cup pecans, chopped
2 garlic cloves, minced

1 teaspoon mustard
2 tablespoons lemon juice
2 tablespoons extra virgin olive oil
Salt and pepper to taste

Directions:

Combine the spinach, pineapple and pecans in a salad bowl.
For the dressing, mix the garlic, mustard, lemon juice and olive oil. Add salt and pepper to taste and mix well.
Drizzle the dressing over the salad.
Serve the salad fresh.

Nutritional information per serving

Calories: 233
Fat: 19.8g

Protein: 2.8g
Carbohydrates: 14.8g

SUPERFOOD SALAD

Time: 20 minutes

Servings: 4

Ingredients:

2 cups baby spinach
1 cup watercress
2 oranges, cut into segments
1 avocado, peeled and cubed
1 cup green grapes, halved
1 teaspoon sherry vinegar

1 teaspoon mustard
1 tablespoon lemon juice
2 tablespoons orange juice
2 tablespoons extra virgin olive oil
Salt and pepper to taste

Directions:

Combine the spinach, watercress, oranges, avocado and grapes in a salad bowl.

For the dressing, mix the vinegar, mustard, lemon juice, orange juice and olive oil in a glass jar. Seal the jar and shake well until creamy.

Drizzle the dressing over the salad and serve it fresh.

Nutritional information per serving

Calories: 236

Fat: 17.4g

Protein: 2.9g

Carbohydrates: 21.3g

GRILLED CHICKEN FENNEL SALAD

Time: 25 minutes

Servings: 4

Ingredients:

2 chicken breasts

Salt and pepper to taste

1 fennel bulb, sliced

2 oranges, cut into segments

1 cup broccoli florets, chopped

1 green onion, sliced

4 tablespoons buttermilk

2 tablespoons lemon juice

1 teaspoon Dijon mustard

½ teaspoon hot sauce

Directions:

Cut the chicken into fillets and season them with salt and pepper.

Heat a grill pan over medium flame. Place the chicken on the grill and cook on each side for 10-15 minutes. Cut the chicken into strips.

Combine the fennel bulb, oranges, broccoli and onion in a salad bowl.

Add the chicken on top.

For the dressing, combine the buttermilk, lemon juice, mustard and hot sauce in a glass jar. Shake the jar well.

Drizzle the dressing over the salad.

Serve the salad fresh.

Nutritional information per serving

Calories: 79

Fat: 0.6g

Protein: 2.9g

Carbohydrates: 17.9g

WILD RICE BELL PEPPERS

Time: 45 minutes

Servings: 6

Ingredients:

2 cups cooked wild rice

1 green onion, chopped

1 shallot, chopped

2 tablespoons chopped cilantro

½ pound ground chicken

Salt and pepper to taste

6 red bell peppers

1 cup diced tomatoes

| 1 cup water | 2 tablespoons lemon juice |
| 1 bay leaf | |

Directions:

Combine the rice, onion, shallot, cilantro, chicken, salt and pepper in a bowl.

Remove the core from the bell peppers.

Stuff the peppers with the rice and chicken mixture and place them in a deep dish baking pan.

Pour in the tomatoes, water, bay leaf and lemon juice and cook on low heat for 30 minutes.

Serve the bell peppers warm.

Nutritional information per serving

| Calories: 308 | Protein: 20.4g |
| Fat: 3.8g | Carbohydrates: 48.9g |

ROASTED SHAVED BRUSSELS SPROUTS

| Time: 30 minutes | Servings: 4 |

Ingredients:

1 pound Brussels sprouts, trimmed and sliced thin

1 pound broccoli, cut into florets	2 tablespoons chopped parsley
2 tablespoons extra virgin olive oil	Salt and pepper to taste
2 tablespoons lemon juice	2 oz. grated Parmesan cheese
1 celery stalk, sliced	

Directions:

Combine the Brussels sprouts, broccoli, oil, lemon juice, celery, parsley, salt and pepper in a bowl and toss around to evenly distribute the ingredients.

Spread them on a baking tray lined with parchment paper.

Bake in the preheated oven at 350F for 25 minutes.

When done, sprinkle with Parmesan and serve right away.

Nutritional information per serving

| Calories: 196 | Protein: 11.8g |
| Fat: 10.9g | Carbohydrates: 18.8g |

PORTOBELLO BURGERS

| Time: 30 minutes | Servings: 2 |

Ingredients:

| 4 Portobello mushrooms | 2 chicken fillets |
| Salt and pepper to taste | 1 teaspoon dried oregano |

3 tablespoons extra virgin olive oil

2 tomato slices

2 lettuce leaves

Directions:

Season the mushrooms with salt and pepper.

Do the same with the chicken, adding dried oregano as well. Drizzle the chicken with olive oil.

Heat a grill pan over medium flame. Place the chicken on the grill and cook on each side until golden and the juices run out clear.

Place the mushrooms on the grill and cook on both sides.

Layer the mushrooms, chicken, tomatoes and lettuce to form the burgers.

Serve the mushroom burgers fresh.

Nutritional information per serving

Calories: 226

Fat: 21.1g

Protein: 6.2g

Carbohydrates: 7.2g

Grapefruit Avocado Salad with Smoked Salmon

Time: 20 minutes

Servings: 4

Ingredients:

2 grapefruits, cut into segments

2 avocados, peeled and sliced

2 cups arugula leaves

8 oz. smoked salmon, sliced

1 lemon, juiced

2 tablespoons extra virgin olive oil

Salt and pepper to taste

Directions:

Combine the grapefruits, avocados, arugula and salmon in a salad bowl.

For the dressing, mix the lemon juice, olive oil, salt and pepper in a bowl until creamy.

Drizzle over the salad and serve fresh.

Nutritional information per serving

Calories: 359

Fat: 29.2g

Protein: 13.1g

Carbohydrates: 15.5g

Roasted Bell Pepper Wild Rice Stew

Time: 35 minutes

Servings: 6

Ingredients:

2 tablespoons extra virgin olive oil

2 shallots, chopped

2 garlic cloves, minced

6 roasted red bell peppers, chopped

1 cup wild rice

2 cups vegetable stock

1 cup diced tomatoes
1 bay leaf

½ teaspoon dried thyme
Salt and pepper to taste

Directions:

Heat the oil in a heavy saucepan. Add the shallots and garlic and cook for 2 minutes.
Add the rest of the ingredients and season with salt and pepper.
Cook on low heat for 25 minutes.
Serve the stew warm and fresh.

Nutritional information per serving

Calories: 172
Fat: 5.1g

Protein: 5.5g
Carbohydrates: 28.5g

Walnut Parsley Pesto Spaghetti

Time: 30 minutes

Servings: 4

Ingredients:

8 oz. whole wheat spaghetti
½ cup walnuts
1½ cups parsley
3 garlic cloves

2 tablespoons lemon juice
4 tablespoons extra virgin olive oil
Salt and pepper to taste

Directions:

Pour a few cups of water in a large pot. Add salt to taste and bring to a boil. Throw in the spaghetti and
cook for 8 minutes until al dente. Drain well.
For the pesto, combine the walnuts, parsley, garlic, lemon juice and olive oil. Add salt and pepper to taste
and pulse in a food processor until the pesto is creamy and smooth.
Mix the pesto with cooked spaghetti and serve right away.

Nutritional information per serving

Calories: 300
Fat: 23.8g

Protein: 7.6g
Carbohydrates: 18.9g

Mixed Barley Salad

Time: 35 minutes

Servings: 4

Ingredients:

1 cup barley
2 cups vegetable stock
1 cup arugula leaves
1 cup broccoli florets, chopped
1 red bell pepper, cored and sliced

1 yellow bell pepper, cored and sliced
2 tablespoons chopped parsley
1 green onion, chopped
1 celery stalk, sliced
2 tablespoons pine nuts

2 tablespoons lemon juice
2 tablespoons orange juice

2 tablespoons extra virgin olive oil
Salt and pepper to taste

Directions:

Combine the barley and stock in a saucepan and cook over low heat for 25 minutes.
Transfer the barley in a salad bowl and stir in the rest of the ingredients.
Season with salt and pepper and mix well.
Serve the salad fresh.

Nutritional information per serving

Calories: 290
Fat: 11.5g

Protein: 8.2g
Carbohydrates: 41.6g

GRILLED LAMB OVER ASPARAGUS SALAD

Time: 30 minutes

Servings: 2

Ingredients:

2 lamb shanks
Salt and pepper to taste
2 tablespoons extra virgin olive oil
1 bunch asparagus

2 tablespoons lemon juice
½ teaspoon hot sauce
2 tablespoons sesame seeds
1 teaspoon soy sauce

Directions:

Season the lamb shanks with salt and pepper and drizzle with olive oil. Rub the oil well into the meat.
Heat a grill pan over medium flame and place the lamb on the grill. Cook on each side for 5-7 minutes.
For the salad, cut the asparagus into fine ribbons using a vegetable peeler. Add the rest of the ingredients
    and mix well. Season with salt and pepper.
Serve the grilled lamb with salad.

Nutritional information per serving

Calories: 365
Fat: 24.8g

Protein: 25.8g
Carbohydrates: 2.7g

AVOCADO LETTUCE CUPS

Time: 20 minutes

Servings: 4

Ingredients:

1 avocado, peeled and diced
1 cup sweet corn, drained
2 tomatoes, diced
2 tablespoons chopped parsley
2 tablespoons chopped cilantro

1 tablespoon balsamic vinegar
Salt and pepper to taste
6 lettuce leaves

Directions:

Combine the avocado, corn, parsley, tomatoes, cilantro and vinegar in a bowl. Season with salt and pepper. Stuff the lettuce leaves with the avocado mixture and serve right away.

Nutritional information per serving

Calories: 147   Protein: 2.6g
Fat: 10.2g   Carbohydrates: 14.6g

Tex Mex Lettuce Cups

Time: 35 minutes   Servings: 6

Ingredients:

1 pound ground pork   1 cucumber, diced
1 shallot, chopped   1 avocado, peeled and diced
1 jalapeño, chopped   2 tablespoons lemon juice
2 garlic cloves, minced   1 tomato, diced
½ teaspoon Tex Mex seasoning   Salt and pepper to taste
2 tablespoons chopped cilantro   6 lettuce leaves

Directions:

Heat a frying pan over medium flame. Add the pork and cook for a few minutes, stirring often.

Add the shallot, jalapeño and garlic and cook for a few more seconds then stir in the Tex Mex seasoning, as well as salt and pepper and cook for about 7 minutes, stirring all the time. Remove from heat and place aside.

For the salsa, combine the cilantro, cucumber, avocado, lemon juice, tomato, salt and pepper.

Stuff the lettuce leaves with the pork mixture and top with the salsa.

Serve the cups fresh.

Nutritional information per serving

Calories: 191   Protein: 21.0g
Fat: 9.3g   Carbohydrates: 6.1g

Fettucine Primavera

Time: 35 minutes   Servings: 6

Ingredients:

12 oz. fettucine   1 bunch asparagus, trimmed and chopped
2 tablespoons extra virgin olive oil   1 zucchini, sliced
2 garlic cloves, minced   ½ cup cream cheese
1 cup green peas   Salt and pepper to taste
1 cup frozen fava beans

Directions:

Pour a few cups of water in a large pot. Add salt to taste and bring to a boil. Throw in the fettucine and cook for 8 minutes then drain well.

Heat the oil in a frying pan. Add the garlic and cook for 30 seconds then add the green peas, fava beans, asparagus and zucchini. Season with salt and pepper and cook for 10 minutes.

Stir in the cream cheese and remove from heat.

Add the cooked fettucine and serve the dish fresh.

Nutritional information per serving

Calories: 367
Fat: 13.7g

Protein: 14.3g
Carbohydrates: 51.0g

Grapefruit Farro Salad

Time: 40 minutes

Servings: 6

Ingredients:

½ cup farro, rinsed
½ cup barley
2 cups vegetable stock
1 pink grapefruit, peeled and cut into segments
2 cups arugula leaves
1 red onion, sliced
1 tablespoon chopped mint

2 tablespoons chopped cilantro
2 tablespoons chopped parsley
1 tablespoon chopped dill
2 tablespoons pine nuts
2 tablespoons lemon juice
1 teaspoon balsamic vinegar
Salt and pepper to taste

Directions:

Combine the farro, barley and stock in a saucepan. Cook on low heat for 20 minutes.

Remove from heat and transfer the farro and barley in a salad bowl.

Add the rest of the ingredients and season with salt and pepper.

Serve the salad right away.

Nutritional information per serving

Calories: 147
Fat: 2.8g

Protein: 5.4g
Carbohydrates: 25.5g

Arugula Raspberry Salad

Time: 20 minutes

Servings: 4

Ingredients:

3 cups arugula leaves
1 cup baby spinach

2 tablespoons pine nuts
2 tablespoons sliced almonds

½ cup chopped parsley
1 avocado, peeled and sliced
2 tablespoons balsamic vinegar

2 tablespoons extra virgin olive oil
Salt and pepper to taste
1 cup fresh raspberries

Directions:

Combine the arugula, baby spinach, pine nuts, almonds, parsley and avocado in a salad bowl.
Drizzle in the vinegar and oil and season with salt and pepper.
Mix gently then top with fresh raspberries.
Serve the salad right away.

Nutritional information per serving

Calories: 234
Fat: 21.6g

Protein: 3.4g
Carbohydrates: 10.6g

MEDITERRANEAN BAKED FISH AND VEGGIES

Time: 30 minutes

Servings: 4

Ingredients:

4 butterfish fillets
Salt and pepper to taste
1 zucchini, sliced
1 eggplant, peeled and sliced
2 red bell peppers, cored and sliced

2 tomatoes, sliced
2 red onions, sliced
2 garlic cloves, minced
3 tablespoons extra virgin olive oil

Directions:

Season the fish with salt and pepper to taste.
Combine the rest of the ingredients in a deep dish baking pan. Add salt and pepper to taste.
Top the vegetables with fish fillets and cook in the preheated oven at 350F for 15 minutes.
Serve the fish warm and fresh.

Nutritional information per serving

Calories: 369
Fat: 12.7g

Protein: 44g
Carbohydrates: 20g

LEEK VEGETABLE BAKE

Time: 40 minutes

Servings: 4

Ingredients:

4 leeks, cut into sticks
½ cup black olives
2 red onions, sliced
4 tomatoes, quartered

1 zucchini, sliced
2 garlic cloves, chopped
½ cup vegetable stock
1 tablespoon lemon juice

1 teaspoon Dijon mustard   Salt and pepper to taste

Directions:

Combine the leeks and the remaining ingredients and season with salt and pepper.
Cook in the preheated oven at 350F for 30 minutes.
Serve the bake warm and fresh.

Nutritional information per serving

Calories: 131   Protein: 3.9g
Fat: 2.8g   Carbohydrates: 26.1g

EGGPLANT BOATS

Time: 40 minutes   Servings: 6

Ingredients:

2 eggplants   ½ teaspoon chili powder
½ pound ground beef   Salt and pepper to taste
2 tablespoons chopped cilantro   1 cup tomato juice
2 garlic cloves, minced   1 cup chicken stock
½ teaspoon cumin powder   1 bay leaf

Directions:

Cut the eggplants in half lengthwise and carefully scoop out the flesh. Chop it finely.
Add the ground beef, cilantro, garlic, cumin powder, chili powder, salt and pepper.
Stuff the eggplants with the beef mixture and place them in a deep dish baking pan.
Pour in the tomato juice and stock then add the bay leaf.
Cook in the preheated oven at 350F for 30 minutes.
Serve the eggplant boats warm and fresh.

Nutritional information per serving

Calories: 128   Protein: 13.8g
Fat: 2.9g   Carbohydrates: 13.3g

LAYERED VEGETABLE BAKE

Time: 1 hour   Servings: 8

Ingredients:

2 red onions, sliced   4 tomatoes, sliced
2 zucchinis, sliced   1 teaspoon dried rosemary
2 eggplants, peeled and sliced   1 teaspoon dried basil
2 red bell peppers, cored and sliced   1 teaspoon dried oregano
2 yellow bell peppers, cored and sliced   Salt and pepper to taste

2 oz. grated Parmesan
1 cup vegetable stock

2 tablespoons extra virgin olive oil

Directions:

Layer the onions, zucchinis, eggplants, bell peppers and tomatoes in a deep dish baking pan, seasoning
with rosemary, basil, oregano, salt and pepper while layering them.
Top with grated Parmesan.
Drizzle in the stock and olive oil and cook in the preheated oven at 350F for 40 minutes.
Serve the vegetables warm and fresh.

Nutritional information per serving

Calories: 137
Fat: 5.7g

Protein: 5.7g
Carbohydrates: 18.8g

BBQ Salmon with Fennel Orange Salad

Time: 40 minutes

Servings: 4

Ingredients:

2 salmon fillets
Salt and pepper to taste
½ teaspoon cumin powder
¼ teaspoon chili powder

¼ cup BBQ sauce
1 fennel bulb, sliced
2 oranges, cut into segments
2 tablespoons extra virgin olive oil

Directions:

Season the salmon with salt, pepper, cumin powder and chili powder. Spread the BBQ sauce over the
fish.
Heat a grill pan over medium flame. Place the fish on the hot grill and cook on each side for 3-4 minutes.
For the salad, mix the fennel, oranges and oil and mix well. Add salt and pepper to taste.
Serve the salmon and salad fresh.

Nutritional information per serving

Calories: 264
Fat: 12.9g

Protein: 18.9g
Carbohydrates: 21.0g

Salmon Chickpea Salad

Time: 30 minutes

Servings: 4

Ingredients:

2 cups vegetable stock
1 celery stalk, sliced
1 shallot, sliced

1 jalapeño pepper, chopped
Salt and pepper to taste
2 salmon fillets, cut into cubes

1 can chickpeas, drained and rinsed
¼ cup chopped parsley
2 tablespoons chopped cilantro

2 tablespoons balsamic vinegar
1 tablespoon lemon juice
2 tablespoons extra virgin olive oil

Directions:

Combine the stock, celery, shallot and jalapeño in a saucepan. Add salt and pepper to taste and bring to a boil.

Add the salmon and cook for 2 minutes. Remove the salmon from the liquid and place in a salad bowl.

Add the chickpeas, parsley, cilantro, vinegar, lemon juice and olive oil.

Adjust the taste with salt and pepper and serve the salad fresh.

Nutritional information per serving

Calories: 370
Fat: 15.6g

Protein: 27.4g
Carbohydrates: 32.0g

WATERCRESS FARRO SALAD

Time: 30 minutes

Servings: 4

Ingredients:

1 cup farro, rinsed
2 cups water
2 Portobello mushrooms, sliced
2 tablespoons extra virgin olive oil
2 cups watercress

1 handful walnuts, chopped
2 tablespoons balsamic vinegar
2 tablespoons extra virgin olive oil
Salt and pepper to taste

Directions:

Combine the farro and water in a saucepan. Cook on low heat for 20 minutes.
When done, transfer the farro in a salad bowl then stir in the rest of the ingredients.
Season with salt and pepper and serve the salad fresh.

Nutritional information per serving

Calories: 350
Fat: 19.5g

Protein: 10.0g
Carbohydrates: 34.6g

BASIL DRESSED CHICKEN SALAD

Time: 30 minutes

Servings: 6

Ingredients:

4 chicken fillets
Salt and pepper to taste
1 teaspoon dried oregano
4 ciabatta slices, cubed

2 tomatoes, cubed
6 basil leaves
2 tablespoons lemon juice
2 tablespoons extra virgin olive oil

Directions:

Season the chicken with salt, pepper and dried oregano.

Heat a grill pan over medium flame and place the chicken on the grill. Cook on each side for 5-6 minutes until golden and the juices run out clean. Cut the chicken into cubes and place them in a salad bowl.

Add the ciabatta and tomatoes as well.

For the dressing, combine the basil, lemon juice and olive oil in a grinding mortar and mix well with the pestle.

Drizzle the dressing over the salad and mix gently.

Serve right away.

Nutritional information per serving

Calories: 420
Fat: 13.8g

Protein: 33.3g
Carbohydrates: 43.0g

MEDITERRANEAN CRUNCHY SALAD

Time: 20 minutes

Servings: 4

Ingredients:

1 zucchini, diced
2 tomatoes, diced
1 cucumber, diced
1 red onion, chopped
½ red pepper, chopped
2 tablespoons chopped parsley
1 garlic clove, minced

1 cup baby spinach leaves
4 basil leaves, chopped
½ teaspoon dried oregano
2 tablespoons extra virgin olive oil
2 tablespoons lemon juice
Salt and pepper to taste

Directions:

Combine the zucchini, tomatoes, cucumber, red onion, red pepper, parsley, garlic, spinach, basil and oregano in a salad bowl.

Stir in the rest of the ingredients and season with salt and pepper.

Serve the salad fresh.

Nutritional information per serving

Calories: 112
Fat: 7.5g

Protein: 2.5g
Carbohydrates: 11.2g

BEAN AND TUNA SALAD

Time: 20 minutes

Servings: 4

Ingredients:

2 cans red beans, drained

1 can water packed tuna, drained

4 tablespoons chopped parsley
1 garlic clove, minced
1 teaspoon lemon zest
1 teaspoon Dijon mustard

2 tablespoons extra virgin olive oil
2 hard-boiled eggs, cubed
2 tablespoons lemon juice
Salt and pepper to taste

Directions:

Combine the red beans and the rest of the ingredients in a salad bowl.

Add salt and pepper to taste and mix well.

Serve the salad right away.

Nutritional information per serving

Calories: 401
Fat: 10.3g

Protein: 23.8g
Carbohydrates: 57.8g

Braised Chicken and Lentils

Time: 45 minutes

Servings: 4

Ingredients:

1 cup brown lentils, rinsed
1 teaspoon cumin powder
½ teaspoon chili powder
1 cup diced tomatoes
4 garlic cloves, chopped
1 shallot, chopped

½ teaspoon dried oregano
½ teaspoon dried thyme
2 cups chicken stock
Salt and pepper to taste
4 chicken breasts

Directions:

Combine the lentils, cumin powder, chili, tomatoes, garlic, shallot, oregano, thyme, stock, salt and pepper
  in a deep dish baking pan.

Place the chicken over the lentils then cover the pan with aluminum foil.

Cook in the preheated oven at 350F for 30 minutes.

Serve the dish warm and fresh.

Nutritional information per serving

Calories: 344
Fat: 11.2g

Protein: 46.1g
Carbohydrates: 13.4g

Feta Beetroot Salad

Time: 20 minutes

Servings: 4

Ingredients:

4 beetroots, cooked, peeled and cubed
8 oz. feta cheese, cubed

1 tablespoon balsamic vinegar
1 pinch chili powder

2 cups arugula leaves

Directions:

Combine all the ingredients in a salad bowl.
Mix well and serve the salad right away.

Nutritional information per serving

Calories: 228
Fat: 12.5g

Protein: 11.2g
Carbohydrates: 19.7g

CREAMY BEETROOT SOUP

Time: 45 minutes

Servings: 6

Ingredients:

3 tablespoons extra virgin olive oil
1 red onion, chopped
2 garlic cloves, minced
4 carrots, sliced
1 celery stalk, sliced
2 potatoes, peeled and cubed

4 beetroots, peeled and cubed
2 cups vegetable stock
2 cups water
1 thyme sprig
Salt and pepper to taste

Directions:

Heat the oil in a soup pot and stir in the onion and garlic. Cook for 30 seconds then add the rest of the
    ingredients.
Cook on low heat for 20 minutes.
When done, remove the thyme sprig and puree the soup with an immersion blender.
Serve the soup warm and fresh.

Nutritional information per serving

Calories: 162
Fat: 7.2g

Protein: 2.9g
Carbohydrates: 23.3g

BROCCOLI PESTO SPAGHETTI

Time: 30 minutes

Servings: 4

Ingredients:

8 oz. whole wheat spaghetti
½ pound broccoli, cut into florets
2 garlic cloves
4 basil leaves

1 tablespoon lemon juice
3 tablespoons extra virgin olive oil
Salt and pepper to taste
Grated Parmesan for serving

Directions:

Pour a few cups of water in a large pot and add a pinch of salt. Bring to a boil then throw in the spaghetti. Cook for 8 minutes then drain well.

For the pesto, combine the broccoli, garlic, basil, lemon juice and olive oil in a food processor. Season with salt and pepper and pulse until ground and well mixed.

Mix the pesto with the cooked spaghetti.

Serve the pasta fresh, topped with grated cheese.

Nutritional information per serving

Calories: 183
Fat: 11.0g

Protein: 4.8g
Carbohydrates: 19.4g

CREAM OF BROCCOLI SOUP

Time: 35 minutes

Servings: 6

Ingredients:

2 tablespoons extra virgin olive oil
2 garlic cloves, minced
1 shallot, chopped
1 pound broccoli, cut into florets
2 potatoes, peeled and cubed

2 cups chicken stock
2 cups water
Salt and pepper to taste
2 oz. grated Parmesan

Directions:

Heat the oil in a soup pot. Add the garlic and shallot and cook for 30 seconds.

Stir in the broccoli, potatoes, stock and water then add salt and pepper to taste.

Cook on low heat for 15 minutes.

When done, add the cheese and puree the soup with an immersion blender.

Serve the soup warm and fresh.

Nutritional information per serving

Calories: 151
Fat: 7.2g

Protein: 6.7g
Carbohydrates: 17.4g

CHUNKY LENTIL VEGETABLE SOUP

Time: 45 minutes

Servings: 8

Ingredients:

3 tablespoons extra virgin olive oil
2 garlic cloves, minced
2 shallots, chopped
1 red bell pepper, cored and diced

1 yellow bell pepper, cored and diced
2 carrots, peeled and sliced
1 zucchini, cubed
2 tomatoes, cubed

⅔ cup brown lentils, rinsed
2 cups vegetable stock
6 cups water
1 bay leaf

½ teaspoon cumin powder
¼ teaspoon chili powder
2 tablespoons lemon juice
Salt and pepper to taste

Directions:

Heat the oil in a soup pot. Add the garlic and shallots and cook for 1 minute.
Stir in the bell peppers, carrots, zucchini, tomatoes, lentils, stock, water, bay leaf, spices and lemon juice.
Season with salt and pepper and cook on low heat for 25-30 minutes.
Serve the soup warm and fresh.

Nutritional information per serving

Calories: 139
Fat: 5.9g

Protein: 5.7g
Carbohydrates: 17.2g

CARROT RIBBON SALAD

Time: 20 minutes

Servings: 4

Ingredients:

1 pound carrots
2 tablespoons extra virgin olive oil
1 teaspoon cumin seeds
1 teaspoon coriander seeds

½ teaspoon chili flakes
1 tablespoon lemon juice
Salt and pepper to taste

Directions:

Cut the carrots into fine ribbons with a vegetable peeler.
Heat the oil in a frying pan and stir in the cumin seeds, coriander seeds and chili flakes. Cook for 30 seconds just until fragrant then remove from heat.
Combine the carrots with the oil and spices then drizzle in the lemon juice then add salt and pepper to taste.
Serve the salad fresh.

Nutritional information per serving

Calories: 109
Fat: 7.2g

Protein: 1.1g
Carbohydrates: 11.5g

SPRING RADISH SALAD

Time: 25 minutes

Servings: 4

Ingredients:

½ pound carrots
½ pound radishes
¼ cup dried cranberries

1 cup baby spinach
1 red onion, sliced
½ red chili, sliced

2 tablespoons lemon juice
2 tablespoons extra virgin olive oil

Salt and pepper to taste

Directions:

Cut the carrots and radishes into fine slices with a vegetable peeler.
Stir in the cranberries, baby spinach, red onion and chili then drizzle in the lemon juice and oil.
Season with salt and pepper and mix well.
Serve the salad fresh.

Nutritional information per serving

Calories: 111
Fat: 7.2g

Protein: 1.4g
Carbohydrates: 11.2g

Asian Chili Chicken Salad

Time: 35 minutes

Servings: 4

Ingredients:

3 oz. bean sprouts
2 cups baby spinach
1 cucumber, cut into sticks
2 green onions, sliced
1 teaspoon chopped mint
1 red chili, sliced

4 chicken fillets
Salt and pepper to taste
1 tablespoon soy sauce
2 tablespoons lemon juice
½ teaspoon miso paste

Directions:

Combine the bean sprouts, baby spinach, cucumber, green onions, mint and red chili in a salad bowl.
Season the chicken with salt and pepper. Heat a grill pan over medium flame and place the chicken on the grill.
Cook on each side for 6-7 minutes until golden and the juices run out clean. Cut into strips.
Top the salad with chicken.
For the dressing, mix the soy sauce, lemon juice and miso paste in a bowl.
Drizzle the mixture over the salad and serve right away.

Nutritional information per serving

Calories: 296
Fat: 10.7g

Protein: 42.9g
Carbohydrates: 5.6g

Ginger Cucumber Salad

Time: 20 minutes

Servings: 4

Ingredients:

4 cucumbers, sliced
½ cup chopped cilantro

1 teaspoon grated ginger
1 garlic clove, minced

1 teaspoon tamarind paste
2 tablespoons hoisin sauce
1 teaspoon soy sauce

2 tablespoons extra virgin olive oil
2 tablespoons sesame seeds

Directions:

Combine the cucumber slices and the cilantro in a salad bowl.

For the dressing, mix the ginger, garlic, tamarind paste, hoisin sauce, soy sauce and olive oil in a bowl.

Drizzle the dressing over the salad and serve right away, topped with sesame seeds.

Nutritional information per serving

Calories: 154
Fat: 9.9g

Protein: 3.2g
Carbohydrates: 16.6g

BROWN LENTIL BUTTERNUT SQUASH SALAD

Time: 45 minutes

Servings: 6

Ingredients:

3 cups butternut squash cubes
Salt and pepper to taste
1 teaspoon cumin powder
½ teaspoon chili powder
½ teaspoon cinnamon powder
2 tablespoons extra virgin olive oil

2 cups cooked lentils
1 orange, cut into segments
2 tablespoons chopped cilantro
2 tablespoons pine nuts
2 tablespoons lemon juice

Directions:

Season the butternut squash with salt, pepper, cumin powder, chili powder and cinnamon then drizzle
    with olive oil and spread the cubes on a baking tray.

Bake in the preheated oven at 350F for 30 minutes.

Combine the cooked lentils, butternut squash, orange segments, cilantro, pine nuts and lemon juice.

Mix well and serve the salad fresh.

Nutritional information per serving

Calories: 323
Fat: 7.5g

Protein: 17.8g
Carbohydrates: 47.8g

BARLEY PRAWN SALAD

Time: 30 minutes

Servings: 4

Ingredients:

1 pound prawns
½ teaspoon chili powder
½ teaspoon cumin powder

1 teaspoon lemon zest
Salt and pepper to taste
3 tablespoons extra virgin olive oil

1 cup barley, rinsed
2 cups vegetable stock
½ cup chopped parsley

2 tablespoons pine nuts
2 tablespoons lemon juice

Directions:

Combine the prawns, chili powder, cumin powder, lemon zest, salt, pepper and olive oil.
Heat a grill pan over medium flame and place the prawns on the grill.
Cook on each side for 1-2 minutes.
In the meantime, cook the barley and stock in a saucepan for 20-25 minutes.
Combine the prawns, cooked barley, parsley, pine nuts and lemon juice in a bowl.
Season with salt and pepper and mix well.
Serve the salad fresh.

Nutritional information per serving

Calories: 426
Fat: 16.7g

Protein: 32.7g
Carbohydrates: 37.6g

BLACK SESAME GRILLED SALMON

Time: 30 minutes

Servings: 2

Ingredients:

2 salmon fillets
Salt and pepper to taste
1 tablespoon soy sauce

2 tablespoons extra virgin olive oil
2 tablespoons black sesame seeds

Directions:

Season the fish with salt and pepper and drizzle it with oil and soy sauce.
Sprinkle with sesame seeds.
Heat a grill pan over medium flame then place the fish on the grill.
Cook on each side for 3-4 minutes.
Serve the salmon fresh and warm.

Nutritional information per serving

Calories: 411
Fat: 29.5g

Protein: 36.6g
Carbohydrates: 2.8g

SALMON GRAPEFRUIT SALAD

Time: 30 minutes

Servings: 4

Ingredients:

4 salmon fillets
Salt and pepper to taste

2 cups arugula leaves
2 grapefruits, cut into segments

1 cup cherry tomatoes, halved   2 tablespoons balsamic vinegar

Directions:

Season the fish with salt and pepper. Heat a grill pan over medium flame and cook on each side for 4-5 minutes.

When done, cut the salmon into cubes and place it in a salad bowl.

Add the rest of the ingredients and adjust the taste with salt and pepper.

Serve the salad fresh.

Nutritional information per serving

Calories: 268   Protein: 35.6g

Fat: 11.2g   Carbohydrates: 7.4g

SAGE BUTTERNUT SQUASH SOUP

Time: 45 minutes   Servings: 6

Ingredients:

2 tablespoons extra virgin olive oil   ½ teaspoon dried sage

1 shallot, chopped   2 cups vegetable stock

2 garlic cloves, chopped   3 cups water

1 red apple, peeled and diced   Salt and pepper to taste

3 cups butternut squash cubes   ½ cup heavy cream

Directions:

Heat the oil in a soup pot over medium flame. Add the shallot and garlic and cook for 30 seconds.

Stir in the rest of the ingredients, except the cream, and cook for 20 minutes.

When done, remove from heat and add the cream.

Puree the soup and serve it warm and fresh.

Nutritional information per serving

Calories: 115   Protein: 1.0g

Fat: 8.5g   Carbohydrates: 10.4g

AVOCADO BUTTERMILK COLD SOUP

Time: 20 minutes   Servings: 6

Ingredients:

2 avocados, peeled and pitted   1 garlic clove

1 cup buttermilk   1 poblano pepper, chopped

2 cups water   Salt and pepper to taste

1 lime, juiced   1 tablespoon chopped chives

2 tablespoons extra virgin olive oil   2 tablespoons chopped cilantro

Directions:

Combine the avocados, buttermilk, water, lime juice, olive oil, garlic and pepper in a blender. Pulse until smooth.

Season with salt and pepper.

Pour the soup into serving bowls and top with chopped chives and cilantro.

Serve the dish fresh and chilled.

Nutritional information per serving

Calories: 200

Fat: 18.1g

Protein: 2.9g

Carbohydrates: 9.8g

Roasted Chestnut Soup

Time: 35 minutes

Servings: 8

Ingredients:

2 tablespoons extra virgin olive oil
1 shallot, chopped
2 garlic cloves, minced
2 cups roasted canned chestnuts
2 cups butternut squash cubes

4 cups chicken stock
2 cups water
½ teaspoon dried thyme
Salt and pepper to taste
½ cup heavy cream

Directions:

Heat the oil in a soup pot and stir in the shallot and garlic. cook for 30 seconds then add the rest of the ingredients, except the cream.

Season with salt and pepper and cook on low heat for 20 minutes.

When done, remove from heat and stir in the cream. Puree the soup with an immersion blender and serve the soup warm.

Nutritional information per serving

Calories: 201

Fat: 6.6g

Protein: 2g

Carbohydrates: 10.2g

Roasted Butternut Squash Soup

Time: 1 hour

Servings: 8

Ingredients:

4 cups butternut squash cubes
2 shallots, halved
4 garlic cloves, halved
3 tablespoons extra virgin olive oil
Salt and pepper to taste

4 cups chicken stock
3 cups water
1 bay leaf
1 thyme sprig
Plain yogurt for serving

Directions:

Combine the butternut squash cubes, shallots and garlic in a baking tray.

Drizzle in the oil and season with salt and pepper.

Cook in the preheated oven at 400F for 25-30 minutes until slightly caramelized.

Transfer the squash in a soup pot and stir in the rest of the ingredients.

Cook for 15 minutes then remove from heat.

Remove the bay leaf and thyme then puree the soup with an immersion blender.

Serve the soup topped with plain yogurt.

Nutritional information per serving

Calories: 83

Fat: 5.5g

Protein: 1g

Carbohydrates: 6.9g

CHICKEN BARLEY SOUP

Time: 50 minutes

Servings: 10

Ingredients:

2 chicken breasts, cut into cubes

4 cups chicken stock

4 cups water

1 shallot, sliced

1 red bell pepper, cored and diced

1 yellow bell pepper, cored and diced

2 carrots, diced

1 parsnip, diced

2 celery stalks, sliced

1 garlic clove, chopped

2 Portobello mushrooms, sliced

1 jalapeño pepper, chopped

1 cup diced tomatoes

¾ cup barley

Salt and pepper to taste

Chopped parsley for serving

Directions:

Combine the chicken, stock and water in a soup pot and cook for 10 minutes.

Add the rest of the ingredients and season with salt and pepper.

Cook on low heat for 30 minutes.

Serve the soup warm, topped with chopped parsley.

Nutritional information per serving

Calories: 145

Fat: 3.7g

Protein: 10.6g

Carbohydrates: 14.1g

GREEN LENTIL STEW

Time: 45 minutes

Servings: 6

Ingredients:

2 tablespoons extra virgin olive oil

2 shallots, chopped

2 garlic cloves, minced

1 carrot, diced

1 celery stalk, diced
½ teaspoon cumin powder
½ teaspoon chili powder
1 cup green lentils
2 cups chicken stock

1 cup diced tomatoes
1 bay leaf
Salt and pepper to taste
2 cups baby spinach
2 tablespoons chopped parsley

Directions:

Heat the oil in a heavy saucepan. Add the shallots and garlic and cook for just 1 minute to soften them.
Add the rest of the ingredients, except the spinach and parsley.
Season with salt and pepper and cook on low to medium heat for 20-25 minutes.
Stir in the baby spinach and parsley and cook for just 1 additional minute.
Serve the stew warm and fresh or chilled.

Nutritional information per serving

Calories: 175
Fat: 5.4g

Protein: 9.4g
Carbohydrates: 23.4g

TOMATO CLAM STEW

Time: 30 minutes

Servings: 6

Ingredients:

2 tablespoons extra virgin olive oil
4 garlic cloves, chopped
1 shallot, chopped
1 pound clams, cleaned
1 pound mussels, cleaned
½ cup dry red wine

½ pound shrimps, peeled and deveined
1 cup diced tomatoes
1 tablespoon lemon juice
1 jalapeño pepper, chopped
Salt and pepper to taste

Directions:

Heat the oil in a heavy saucepan and add the garlic and shallot. Cook for 1 minute until softened then stir
in the clams, mussels, red wine, shrimps, tomatoes, lemon juice and pepper.
Season with salt and pepper and cook for 10 minutes.
Serve the stew fresh.

Nutritional information per serving

Calories: 214
Fat: 7.2g

Protein: 18.6g
Carbohydrates: 14.5g

ROASTED GARLIC SOUP

Time: 1 hour

Servings: 6

Ingredients:

1 pound garlic

2 tablespoons olive oil

2 shallots, chopped
¼ cup dry white wine
2 cups chicken stock
2 cups water

2 potatoes, peeled and cubed
½ cup low fat milk
Salt and pepper to taste

Directions:

Wrap the garlic in tinfoil and place in a baking tray. Cook in the preheated oven at 350F for 30 minutes.
When done, unwrap the garlic and carefully remove the skins.
Place the garlic in a soup pot and stir in the oil, shallots, wine, stock, water, potatoes, milk, salt and pepper.
Cook in the preheated oven at 350F for 20 minutes.
When done, puree the soup with an immersion blender and serve it warm or chilled.

Nutritional information per serving

Calories: 224
Fat: 5.5g

Protein: 7.0g
Carbohydrates: 38.2g

Leek Black Olive Stew

Time: 40 minutes

Servings: 6

Ingredients:

2 tablespoons extra virgin olive oil
6 leeks, cut into thick slices
2 cups diced tomatoes
¼ cup dry white wine
1 cup chicken stock

1 bay leaf
1 thyme sprig
1 cup black olives
Salt and pepper to taste

Directions:

Heat the oil in a saucepan.
Add the leeks, tomatoes, wine, stock, bay leaf, thyme sprig, black olives, salt and pepper.
Cook on low heat for 30 minutes.
Serve the stew warm.

Nutritional information per serving

Calories: 143
Fat: 7.6g

Protein: 2.2g
Carbohydrates: 16.9g

Creamy Fennel Soup

Time: 40 minutes

Servings: 8

Ingredients:

2 tablespoons extra virgin olive oil
1 fennel bulb, sliced
1 shallot, sliced

2 garlic cloves, minced
2 potatoes, peeled and cubed
2 cups chicken stock

4 cups water
1 tablespoon lemon juice
1 teaspoon lemon zest

Salt and pepper to taste
1 cup baby spinach

Directions:

Combine the oil, fennel, shallot, garlic, potatoes, stock, water, lemon juice and zest in a saucepan.
Season with salt and pepper and cook for 20 minutes. Add the spinach and cook for 2 additional minutes.
When done, puree the soup with an immersion blender.
Serve the soup warm or chilled.

Nutritional information per serving

Calories: 82
Fat: 3.8g

Protein: 1.6g
Carbohydrates: 11.4g

SUMMER SQUASH CORN CHOWDER

Time: 45 minutes

Servings: 8

Ingredients:

2 tablespoons extra virgin olive oil
1 shallot, chopped
2 garlic cloves, chopped
1 celery stalk, sliced
2 summer squashes, sliced
½ pound frozen sweet corn

2 cups chicken stock
2 cups low fat milk
1 thyme sprig
1 potato, peeled and cubed
Salt and pepper to taste

Directions:

Combine the oil and the remaining ingredients in a soup pot.
Season with salt and pepper and cook on low heat for 30 minutes.
Serve the soup warm or chilled.

Nutritional information per serving

Calories: 103
Fat: 4.4g

Protein: 3.6g
Carbohydrates: 13.8g

BEAN AND PASTA SOUP

Time: 45 minutes

Servings: 8

Ingredients:

2 tablespoons extra virgin olive oil
1 shallot, chopped
2 garlic cloves, chopped
2 red bell peppers, cored and diced
1 celery stalk, sliced

1 zucchini, cubed
1 cup diced tomatoes
1 can black beans, drained
1 can cannellini beans, drained
½ teaspoon dried basil

½ teaspoon dried oregano
1 cup short pasta
2 cups vegetable stock

6 cups water
2 tablespoons lemon juice
Salt and pepper to taste

Directions:

Heat the oil in a soup pot and stir in the shallot and garlic. Cook for 30 seconds then add the rest of the ingredients.

Season with salt and pepper and simmer on low heat for 35-40 minutes.

Serve the soup warm and fresh.

Nutritional information per serving

Calories: 252
Fat: 4.5g

Protein: 13.1g
Carbohydrates: 41.3g

REEK LENTIL SOUP

Time: 40 minutes

Servings: 8

Ingredients:

1 cup brown lentils
¼ cup red lentils
2 garlic cloves, minced
1 shallot, chopped
½ teaspoon dried oregano
1 teaspoon dried basil
½ teaspoon dried rosemary

1 cup diced tomatoes
1 carrot, diced
1 jalapeño pepper, chopped
2 cups vegetable stock
4 cups water
Salt and pepper to taste

Directions:

Combine the lentils, garlic, shallot and the remaining ingredients in a saucepan.
Season with salt and pepper to taste and cook on low heat for 25-30 minutes.
Serve the soup warm and fresh.

Nutritional information per serving

Calories: 47
Fat: 0.2g

Protein: 2.8g
Carbohydrates: 8.6g

EMON CREAM OF ASPARAGUS SOUP

Time: 40 minutes

Servings: 8

Ingredients:

2 tablespoons extra virgin olive oil
2 garlic cloves, chopped
1 shallot, chopped
2 cups chicken stock

2 cups water
2 pounds asparagus, trimmed and sliced
1 potato, peeled and cubed
1 pinch nutmeg

1 tablespoon lemon juice
1 teaspoon grated lemon zest

Salt and pepper to taste

Directions:

Heat the oil in a soup pot and stir in the garlic and shallot. Cook for 30 seconds then add the rest of the ingredients.

Season with salt and pepper and cook on low heat for 20 minutes.

When done, pour the soup into a blender and puree until smooth.

Serve the soup warm and fresh.

Nutritional information per serving

Calories: 74
Fat: 3.8g

Protein: 3.2g
Carbohydrates: 8.9g

JAMAICAN CHICKEN STEW

Time: 1 hour

Servings: 8

Ingredients:

2 tablespoons extra virgin olive oil
4 chicken breasts, halved
2 shallots, sliced
4 garlic cloves, minced
1 teaspoon curry powder
1 teaspoon dried thyme
½ teaspoon chili powder
1 pinch nutmeg

½ cup dry red wine
1 teaspoon capers, chopped
1 can black beans, drained
1 can diced tomatoes
1 cup chicken stock
1 bay leaf
Salt and pepper to taste

Directions:

Heat the oil in a heavy saucepan and add the chicken. Cook on all sides until browned then stir in the rest of the ingredients and season with salt and pepper.

Cook on low heat for 35-40 minutes.

Serve the stew warm and fresh.

Nutritional information per serving

Calories: 285
Fat: 9.2g

Protein: 25.9g
Carbohydrates: 16.9g

ROSEMARY SPLIT PEA SOUP

Time: 1 hour

Servings: 8

Ingredients:

2 tablespoons extra virgin olive oil
2 shallots, chopped

4 garlic cloves, minced
2 carrots, diced

½ teaspoon smoked paprika
4 cups water
2 cups vegetable stock
1½ cups split peas, rinsed

½ cup diced tomatoes
2 rosemary sprigs
Salt and pepper to taste

Directions:

Heat the oil in a heavy saucepan and stir in the shallots and garlic. Cook for 1 minute then add the rest of the ingredients.

Season with salt and pepper and cook on low heat for 30-35 minutes.

Serve the soup warm and fresh.

Nutritional information per serving

Calories: 171
Fat: 4.0g

Protein: 9.6g
Carbohydrates: 25.6g

CREAMY CELERY SOUP

Time: 40 minutes

Servings: 6

Ingredients:

2 tablespoons extra virgin olive oil
2 shallots, chopped
2 celery roots, peeled and cubed
3 potatoes, peeled and cubed

2 cups vegetable stock
2 cups water
Salt and pepper to taste
¼ cup heavy cream

Directions:

Heat the oil in a soup pot and stir in the shallots. Cook for 2 minutes until softened.

Add the rest of the ingredients, except the cream, and season with salt and pepper.

Cook on low heat for 20 minutes.

When done, remove from heat, puree the soup with an immersion blender. Stir in cream.

Serve the soup warm and fresh.

Nutritional information per serving

Calories: 157
Fat: 6.8g

Protein: 2.9g
Carbohydrates: 22.5g

POTATO BEEF SOUP

Time: 1 hour

Servings: 10

Ingredients:

2 tablespoons extra virgin olive
2 pounds beef roast, cubed
2 cups beef stock
6 cups water

2 celery stalks, sliced
2 carrots, sliced
4 potatoes, peeled and cubed
2 tomatoes, diced

1 thyme sprig
1 rosemary sprig
½ teaspoon dried oregano

Salt and pepper to taste
Lemon juice for serving

Directions:

Heat the oil in a soup pot and stir in the beef roast. Cook for a few minutes on all sides then add the stock and water.

Cook on medium heat for 20 minutes.

Add the rest of the ingredients and season with salt and pepper.

Cook for 20 additional minutes.

Serve the soup warm and fresh, drizzled with lemon juice.

Nutritional information per serving

Calories: 265
Fat: 8.7g

Protein: 29.9g
Carbohydrates: 15.8g

SPICY COCONUT MUSSELS

Time: 35 minutes

Servings: 8

Ingredients:

2 tablespoons extra virgin olive oil
2 garlic cloves, minced
1 cup coconut milk
2 tablespoons red curry paste
½ teaspoon grated ginger

1 cup chicken stock
1 lemongrass stalk, crushed
1 bay leaf
4 pounds mussels, cleaned and rinsed

Directions:

Heat the oil in a saucepan and add the garlic. Cook for 30 seconds then stir in the coconut milk, curry paste, ginger, stock, lemongrass stalk and bay leaf.

Cook for 5 minutes then add the mussels.

Cook for a few additional minutes then serve right away.

Nutritional information per serving

Calories: 312
Fat: 17.0g

Protein: 27.8g
Carbohydrates: 11.3g

CHICKEN CASSOULET

Time: 1 hour

Servings: 8

Ingredients:

2 tablespoons extra virgin olive oil
2 chicken breasts, cubed
1 celery stalk, sliced

2 carrots, diced
2 cups butternut squash cubes
1 can white beans, drained

½ teaspoon dried oregano
1 thyme sprig
2 cups chicken stock

2 cups water
Salt and pepper to taste

Directions:

Heat the oil in a heavy saucepan.
Add the chicken and cook for a few minutes on all sides until golden.
Stir in the celery, carrots, butternut squash, beans, oregano, thyme, stock and water, as well as salt and pepper.
Cook on low heat for 30 minutes.
Serve the cassoulet warm and fresh.

Nutritional information per serving

Calories: 200
Fat: 6.4g

Protein: 16.6g
Carbohydrates: 19.5g

Beef and Barley Oven Cooked Stew

Time: 2 hours

Servings: 10

Ingredients:

1½ pounds beef roast, cubed
2 shallots, chopped
4 garlic cloves, minced
2 carrots, sliced
2 celery stalks, sliced
2 turnips, peeled and diced
1 parsnip, diced
1 cup pearl barley, rinsed

1 pound button mushrooms
1 cup diced tomatoes
2 cups beef stock
1 cup water
1 thyme sprig
1 bay leaf
1 rosemary sprig
Salt and pepper to taste

Directions:

Combine the beef roast and the rest of the ingredients in a heavy saucepan that can go in the oven.
Season with salt and pepper and cover the pot with a lid.
Cook in the preheated oven at 300F for 1½ hours.
Serve the stew warm and fresh.

Nutritional information per serving

Calories: 240
Fat: 4.8g

Protein: 25.4g
Carbohydrates: 23.9g

Lemon Mint Pea Soup

Time: 40 minutes

Servings: 8

Ingredients:

2 tablespoons extra virgin olive oil

1 shallot, chopped

2 garlic cloves, minced
4 cups green peas
1 teaspoon dried mint
4 cups vegetable stock

1 tablespoon lemon juice
1 teaspoon lemon zest
Salt and pepper to taste

Directions:

Heat the oil in a soup pot and stir in the shallot and garlic. Cook for 1 minute until softened then add the rest of the ingredients.

Season with salt and pepper and cook for 20 minutes.

When done, remove from heat and puree the soup with a blender.

Serve the soup warm.

Nutritional information per serving

Calories: 95
Fat: 3.9g

Protein: 4.2g
Carbohydrates: 11.5g

WILD RICE MUSHROOM SOUP

Time: 45 minutes

Servings: 8

Ingredients:

2 tablespoons extra virgin olive oil
4 garlic cloves, minced
1 shallot, chopped
1 celery stalk, sliced
1 parsnip, diced
1 teaspoon dried thyme

1 pound wild mushrooms, chopped
2 chicken breasts, cubed
½ cup wild rice
2 cups chicken stock
6 cups water
Salt and pepper to taste

Directions:

Heat the oil in a soup pot and stir in the garlic and shallot. Cook for 1 minute until softened.

Add the celery, parsnip, thyme, mushrooms, chicken, rice, stock and water.

Season with salt and pepper and cook on low heat for 30-35 minutes.

Serve the soup warm and fresh.

Nutritional information per serving

Calories: 163
Fat: 6.6g

Protein: 13.9g
Carbohydrates: 13.4g

CREAM OF LEEK SOUP

Time: 40 minutes

Servings: 8

Ingredients:

2 tablespoons extra virgin olive oil
6 leeks, sliced
1 celery root, peeled and cubed

2 potatoes, peeled and cubed
2 cups vegetable stock
4 cups water

1 thyme sprig   Salt and pepper to taste
1 rosemary sprig   ½ cup heavy cream

Directions:

Heat the oil in a soup pot.
Add the leeks and celery and cook for a few minutes until softened.
Stir in the potatoes, stock, water, thyme, rosemary, salt and pepper.
Cook on low heat for 25 minutes.
When done, remove from heat and stir in the cream.
Puree the soup with an immersion blender.
Serve the soup warm or chilled.

Nutritional information per serving

Calories: 143   Protein: 2.4g
Fat: 6.6g   Carbohydrates: 20.1g

COLD TOMATO SOUP

Time: 25 minutes   Servings: 4

Ingredients:

1 pound fresh tomatoes, peeled and diced   1 cup water
1 cucumber, sliced   ½ cup plain yogurt
1 shallot, sliced   Salt and pepper to taste
1 jalapeño pepper, chopped   2 tablespoons chopped parsley for
1 garlic clove   serving

Directions:

Combine the tomatoes and the rest of the ingredients in a blender and pulse until smooth.
Pour into serving bowls and top with chopped parsley.
Serve the soup fresh.

Nutritional information per serving

Calories: 58   Protein: 3.5g
Fat: 0.7g   Carbohydrates: 10.3g

BOUILLABAISSE

Time: 45 minutes   Servings: 8

Ingredients:

2 tablespoons extra virgin olive oil   2 carrots, sliced
2 shallots, chopped   4 tomatoes, peeled and diced
2 garlic cloves, chopped   1 cup tomato juice
1 celery stalk, sliced   ¼ cup dry white wine

1 thyme sprig
1 bay leaf
Salt and pepper to taste

1 pound mussels, cleaned and rinsed
1 pound clams, cleaned
4 halibut fillets, cubed

Directions:

Heat the oil in a large pot and stir in the shallots and garlic. Cook for 1 minute then add the celery, carrots, tomatoes, tomato juice, white wine, thyme and bay leaf.

Season with salt and pepper and cook for 10 minutes on low heat.

Add the mussels, clams and halibut and cook for 10 additional minutes.

Serve the dish warm and fresh.

Nutritional information per serving

Calories: 297
Fat: 8.4g

Protein: 38.4g
Carbohydrates: 14.5g

SPICY FISH CHOWDER

Time: 40 minutes

Servings: 8

Ingredients:

3 tablespoons extra virgin olive oil
1 sweet onion, chopped
2 carrots, diced
1 celery stalk, diced
2 garlic cloves, chopped
2 tablespoons tomato paste
½ cup dry white wine

2 large potatoes, peeled and cubed
2 cups water
2 cups vegetable stock
1 cup clam juice
1 can diced tomatoes
Salt and pepper to taste
2 pounds halibut fillets, cubed

Directions:

Heat the oil in a large soup pot and stir in the onion, carrots, celery, garlic and tomato paste. Cook for 2 minutes.

Add the rest of the ingredients, except the fish, and season as needed.

Cook over low heat for 15 minutes.

Add the fish and cook for 10 additional minutes.

Serve the chowder fresh and warm.

Nutritional information per serving

Calories: 193
Fat: 5.5g

Protein: 2.7g
Carbohydrates: 22.3g

Greek Cold Cucumber Soup

Time: 20 minutes

Servings: 6

Ingredients:

4 cucumbers
2 cups plain yogurt
2 garlic cloves

2 tablespoons lemon juice
Salt and pepper to taste
2 tablespoons chopped dill

Directions:

Combine the cucumbers, yogurt, garlic, lemon juice, salt and pepper in a blender. Pulse until smooth. Stir in the dill and serve the soup chilled.

Nutritional information per serving

Calories: 94
Fat: 1.3g

Protein: 6.3g
Carbohydrates: 14.1g

White Bean Artichoke Salad

Time: 40 minutes

Servings: 6

Ingredients:

1 cup uncooked spelt, rinsed
2 cups water
1 teaspoon dried mint
½ cup chopped parsley
1 red onion, sliced

6 artichoke hearts, chopped
1 can white beans, drained
2 tablespoons lemon juice
2 tablespoons olive oil
Salt and pepper to taste

Directions:

Combine the spelt and water in a saucepan. Cook on low heat until the water has absorbed the liquid.
Transfer the spelt in a salad bowl and stir in the rest of the ingredients.
Mix well and season with salt and pepper to taste.
Serve the salad fresh.

Nutritional information per serving

Calories: 325
Fat: 6.0g

Protein: 16.2g
Carbohydrates: 56.1g

Curried Chicken Salad

Time: 30 minutes

Servings: 6

Ingredients:

2 chicken breasts

2 celery stalks, sliced

1 green apple, peeled and diced
¼ cup raisins
1 avocado, peeled and pitted
1 lime, juiced

2 garlic cloves
2 tablespoons green curry paste
Salt and pepper to taste

Directions:

Cook the chicken in a large pot of water.
Drain and chop it into small cubes. Place in a salad bowl.
Add the celery, apple and raisins.
For the sauce, combine the avocado, lime juice, garlic and curry paste in a blender. Pulse until smooth.
Add the dressing into the bowl and mix well.
Season with salt and pepper and serve the salad fresh.

Nutritional information per serving

Calories: 208
Fat: 11.1g

Protein: 14.5g
Carbohydrates: 13.9g

Chili Chicken Pasta Salad

Time: 25 minutes

Servings: 6

Ingredients:

10 oz. pasta of your choice, cooked and drained
2 chicken breasts, cooked and cubed
1 cup sweet corn, drained
1 red chili, chopped
1 jalapeño pepper, chopped
2 green onions, chopped

2 cups cherry tomatoes, halved
2 tablespoons lemon juice
2 tablespoons extra virgin olive oil
Salt and pepper to taste

Directions:

Combine the pasta with the chicken and the rest of the ingredients.
Season with salt and pepper and mix well.
Serve the salad fresh.

Nutritional information per serving

Calories: 239
Fat: 8.9g

Protein: 17.6g
Carbohydrates: 22.6g

Arugula Gorgonzola Salad

Time: 15 minutes

Servings: 4

Ingredients:

4 cups arugula
2 beef steaks, cooked and cut into thin strips

2 oranges, cut into segments

1 lime, juiced

2 tablespoons extra virgin olive oil

2 garlic cloves, minced

Salt and pepper to taste

3 oz. gorgonzola cheese, crumbled

Directions:

Combine the arugula, oranges and beef in a salad bowl.

Combine the lime juice, oil and garlic in a bowl and mix well.

Drizzle the dressing over the salad and season with salt and pepper. Mix well.

Top with cheese and serve the salad fresh.

Nutritional information per serving

Calories: 268

Fat: 15.9g

Protein: 19.1g

Carbohydrates: 15.2g

Chicken Tabbouleh

Time: 30 minutes

Servings: 4

Ingredients:

⅔ cup quinoa, rinsed

1¾ cups chicken stock

1 cup chopped parsley

¼ cup chopped cilantro

1 cucumber, diced

4 mint leaves, chopped

1 cup cherry tomatoes, quartered

1 chicken breast, cooked and diced

2 tablespoons lemon juice

Salt and pepper to taste

Directions:

Combine the quinoa and stock in a saucepan. Cook until the liquid has been completely absorbed.

Transfer the quinoa in a salad bowl and add the rest of the ingredients and season with salt and pepper.

Serve the salad fresh.

Nutritional information per serving

Calories: 211

Fat: 3.9g

Protein: 19.9g

Carbohydrates: 25.1g

Chipotle Avocado Tortilla Wraps

Time: 30 minutes

Servings: 4

Ingredients:

1 chicken breast, cooked and shredded

1 avocado, sliced

2 chipotle peppers, chopped

½ cup chopped cilantro

1 lime, juiced

1 cup arugula

2 green onions, sliced

Salt and pepper to taste

2 flour tortillas

Directions:

Combine the chicken, avocado, chipotle peppers, cilantro, lime, arugula and green onions in a salad bowl. Season with salt and pepper.

Fill each tortilla with the salad and serve right away.

Nutritional information per serving

Calories: 218

Fat: 11.8g

Protein: 16.3g

Carbohydrates: 14.4g

ASIAN STYLE GREEN BEAN SALAD

Time: 20 minutes

Servings: 4

Ingredients:

Salt to taste
1 pound green beans, trimmed
1 celery stalk, sliced
2 green onions, sliced
2 tablespoons chopped cilantro
1 tablespoon rice wine vinegar

2 tablespoons soy sauce
2 tablespoons sesame seeds
1 teaspoon sesame oil
2 garlic cloves, minced
1 jalapeño pepper, chopped

Directions:

Pour a few cups of water in a pot. Add salt to taste and bring it to a boil.

Throw in beans and cook for 2 minutes then drain well and place in a salad bowl.

Stir in the celery, green onions and cilantro.

For the dressing, combine the vinegar, soy sauce, sesame seeds, sesame oil, garlic and pepper in a bowl.

Drizzle the dressing over the salad and serve right away.

Nutritional information per serving

Calories: 84

Fat: 3.6g

Protein: 3.7g

Carbohydrates: 11.2g

ROASTED RED PEPPER SALAD

Time: 20 minutes

Servings: 4

Ingredients:

8 roasted red bell peppers, chopped
2 garlic cloves, minced
½ lettuce head, shredded

3 tablespoons balsamic vinegar
2 tablespoons extra virgin olive oil
Salt and pepper to taste

Directions:

Combine the bell peppers, garlic, lettuce, vinegar, oil, salt and pepper in a salad bowl.

Mix well and serve the salad fresh.

Nutritional information per serving

Calories: 120

Fat: 7.1g

Protein: 2.3g

Carbohydrates: 13.8g

Garden Citrus Salad

Time: 25 minutes

Servings: 4

Ingredients:

2 cups baby spinach
2 cups arugula leaves
1 zucchini, sliced
1 red onion, sliced
2 tablespoons chopped cilantro

1 orange, cut into segments
1 lime, juiced
2 tablespoons extra virgin olive oil
Salt and pepper to taste

Directions:

Combine the baby spinach, arugula leaves, zucchini, red onion, cilantro and orange in a salad bowl. Drizzle in the lime juice and oil then season with salt and pepper.
Serve the salad fresh.

Nutritional information per serving

Calories: 112

Fat: 7.3g

Protein: 2.1g

Carbohydrates: 12.3g

Herbed White Bean Salad

Time: 20 minutes

Servings: 6

Ingredients:

2 cans white beans, drained
½ cup chopped parsley
½ cup chopped cilantro
1 teaspoon dried basil
1 teaspoon dried oregano

1 teaspoon dried thyme
½ lemon, juiced
2 tablespoons extra virgin olive oil
Salt and pepper to taste

Directions:

Combine the white beans, parsley, cilantro, herbs, lemon juice and olive oil.
Season with salt and pepper and mix well.
Serve the salad fresh.

Nutritional information per serving

Calories: 278

Fat: 5.3g

Protein: 16g

Carbohydrates: 41.2g

HERBED TURKEY BURGERS

Time: 30 minutes

Servings: 4

Ingredients:

1 pound ground turkey
1 potato, peeled and grated
1 chipotle pepper, chopped
1 shallot, chopped
4 garlic cloves, minced
1 tablespoon chopped cilantro

1 tablespoon chopped parsley
½ teaspoon dried oregano
½ teaspoon dried basil
½ teaspoon cumin powder
Salt and pepper to taste
Toppings of your choice

Directions:

Combine the ground turkey, vegetables, herbs and spices in a bowl. Mix well then season with salt and pepper. Form 4 burgers.
Heat a grill pan over medium to high heat and place the burgers on the hot pan.
Cook on each side for 4-5 minutes.
Serve the burgers with your favorite toppings.

Nutritional information per serving

Calories: 267
Fat: 12.6g

Protein: 32.5g
Carbohydrates: 10.2g

ORIENTAL RICE SALAD

Time: 40 minutes

Servings: 6

Ingredients:

1 cup wild rice
2 cups vegetable stock
1 teaspoon dried mint
¼ cup chopped parsley
½ teaspoon cumin powder

1 can chickpeas, drained
¼ cup raisins
Salt and pepper to taste
2 tablespoons extra virgin olive oil
2 tablespoons lemon juice

Directions:

Combine the rice and stock in a saucepan and cook on low heat for 20 minutes until the liquid has been all absorbed.
Transfer the rice in a salad bowl.
Add the rest of the ingredients and season with salt and pepper.
Mix the salad fresh.

Nutritional information per serving

Calories: 280
Fat: 7.1g

Protein: 10.8g
Carbohydrates: 45.7g

BLACK BEAN QUINOA SALAD

Time: 30 minutes

Servings: 6

Ingredients:

1 cup quinoa, rinsed
2 cups vegetable stock
2 tomatoes, diced
2 green onions, sliced
1 can black beans, drained

2 tablespoons chopped cilantro
2 tablespoons lemon juice
2 tablespoons extra virgin olive oil
Salt and pepper to taste

Directions:

Combine the quinoa and stock in a saucepan.
Cook for 20-25 minutes until the liquid has been absorbed.
Transfer the quinoa in a salad bowl and stir in the rest of the ingredients.
Adjust the taste with salt and pepper and serve the salad fresh.

Nutritional information per serving

Calories: 267
Fat: 7.0g

Protein: 11.6g
Carbohydrates: 40.7g

Dinner Recipes

Zucchini Salmon Salad

Time: 30 minutes

Servings: 4

Ingredients:

2 salmon fillets
2 tablespoons soy sauce
2 zucchinis, sliced
Salt and pepper to taste

2 tablespoons extra virgin olive oil
2 tablespoons sesame seeds
Salt and pepper to taste

Directions:

Drizzle the salmon with soy sauce.

Heat a grill pan over medium flame. Place the salmon on the grill and cook on each side for 2-3 minutes.

Season the zucchini with salt and pepper and place it on the grill as well. Cook for a few minutes on each side until golden.

Place the zucchini, salmon and the rest of the ingredients in a bowl.

Serve the salad fresh.

Nutritional information per serving

Calories: 224
Fat: 14.9g

Protein: 19.8g
Carbohydrates: 5.0g

Pan Fried Salmon

Time: 20 minutes

Servings: 4

Ingredients:

4 salmon fillets
Salt and pepper to taste
1 teaspoon dried oregano

1 teaspoon dried basil
3 tablespoons extra virgin olive oil

Directions:

Season the fish with salt, pepper, oregano and basil.

Heat the oil in a pan and place the salmon in the hot oil, with the skin facing down.

Fry on each side for 2 minutes until golden brown and fragrant.

Serve the salmon warm and fresh.

Nutritional information per serving

Calories: 327
Fat: 21.5g

Protein: 34.6g
Carbohydrates: 0.3g

GRILLED SALMON WITH PINEAPPLE SALSA

Time: 30 minutes   Servings: 4

Ingredients:

4 salmon fillets
Salt and pepper to taste
2 tablespoons Cajun seasoning
1 fresh pineapple, peeled and diced
1 cup cherry tomatoes, quartered
2 tablespoons chopped cilantro

2 tablespoons chopped parsley
1 teaspoon dried mint
2 tablespoons lemon juice
2 tablespoons extra virgin olive oil
1 teaspoon honey
Salt and pepper to taste

Directions:

Season the fish with salt, pepper and Cajun seasoning.
Heat a grill pan over medium flame. Place the fish on the grill and cook on each side for 3-4 minutes.
For the salsa, mix the pineapple, tomatoes, cilantro, parsley, mint, lemon juice and honey in a bowl.
    Season with salt and pepper.
Serve the grilled salmon with the pineapple salsa.

Nutritional information per serving

Calories: 332   Protein: 35.4g
Fat: 18.2g   Carbohydrates: 9.0g

MEDITERRANEAN CHICKPEA SALAD

Time: 20 minutes   Servings: 6

Ingredients:

1 can chickpeas, drained
1 fennel bulb, sliced
1 red onion, sliced
1 teaspoon dried basil
1 teaspoon dried oregano

2 tablespoons chopped parsley
4 garlic cloves, minced
2 tablespoons lemon juice
2 tablespoons extra virgin olive oil
Salt and pepper to taste

Directions:

Combine the chickpeas, fennel, red onion, herbs, garlic, lemon juice and oil in a salad bowl.
Season with salt and pepper and serve the salad fresh.

Nutritional information per serving

Calories: 200   Protein: 7.4g
Fat: 7.9g   Carbohydrates: 25.8g

Warm Chorizo Chickpea Salad

Time: 20 minutes

Servings: 6

Ingredients:

1 tablespoon extra virgin olive oil
4 chorizo links, sliced
1 red onion, sliced
4 roasted red bell peppers, chopped

1 can chickpeas, drained
2 cups cherry tomatoes
2 tablespoons balsamic vinegar
Salt and pepper to taste

Directions:

Heat the oil in a skillet and add the chorizo. Cook briefly just until fragrant then add the onion, bell peppers and chickpeas and cook for 2 additional minutes.

Transfer the mixture in a salad bowl then add the tomatoes, vinegar, salt and pepper.

Mix well and serve the salad right away.

Nutritional information per serving

Calories: 359
Fat: 19.8g

Protein: 17.5g
Carbohydrates: 29.1g

Greek Roasted Fish

Time: 30 minutes

Servings: 4

Ingredients:

4 salmon fillets
1 tablespoon chopped oregano
1 teaspoon dried basil
1 zucchini, sliced
1 red onion, sliced

1 carrot, sliced
1 lemon, sliced
2 tablespoons extra virgin olive oil
Salt and pepper to taste

Directions:

Combine all the ingredients in a deep dish baking pan.

Season with salt and pepper and cook in the preheated oven at 350F for 20 minutes.

Serve the fish and vegetables warm.

Nutritional information per serving

Calories: 328
Fat: 18.3g

Protein: 35.8g
Carbohydrates: 7.8g

ᴛOMATO FISH BAKE

Time: 30 minutes

Servings: 4

Ingredients:

4 cod fillets
4 tomatoes, sliced
4 garlic cloves, minced
1 shallot, sliced

1 celery stalk, sliced
1 teaspoon fennel seeds
1 cup vegetable stock
Salt and pepper to taste

Directions:

Layer the cod fillets and tomatoes in a deep dish baking pan.
Add the rest of the ingredients and season with salt and pepper.
Cook in the preheated oven at 350F for 20 minutes.
Serve the dish warm or chilled.

Nutritional information per serving

Calories: 299
Fat: 3.3g

Protein: 61.4g
Carbohydrates: 6.2g

ɢARLICKY TOMATO CHICKEN CASSEROLE

Time: 50 minutes

Servings: 4

Ingredients:

4 chicken breasts
2 tomatoes, sliced
1 can diced tomatoes
2 garlic cloves, chopped
1 shallot, chopped

1 bay leaf
1 thyme sprig
½ cup dry white wine
½ cup chicken stock
Salt and pepper to taste

Directions:

Combine the chicken and the rest of the ingredients in a deep dish baking pan.
Adjust the taste with salt and pepper and cover the pot with a lid or aluminum foil.
Cook in the preheated oven at 330F for 40 minutes.
Serve the casserole warm.

Nutritional information per serving

Calories: 313
Fat: 10.8g

Protein: 41.7g
Carbohydrates: 5.6g

CHICKEN CACCIATORE

Time: 45 minutes

Servings: 6

Ingredients:

2 tablespoons extra virgin olive oil
6 chicken thighs
1 sweet onion, chopped
2 garlic cloves, minced
2 red bell peppers, cored and diced
2 carrots, diced
1 rosemary sprig

1 thyme sprig
4 tomatoes, peeled and diced
½ cup tomato juice
¼ cup dry white wine
1 cup chicken stock
1 bay leaf
Salt and pepper to taste

Directions:

Heat the oil in a heavy saucepan.
Add the chicken and cook on all sides until golden.
Stir in the onion and garlic and cook for 2 minutes.
Stir in the rest of the ingredients and season with salt and pepper.
Cook on low heat for 30 minutes.
Serve the chicken cacciatore warm and fresh.

Nutritional information per serving

Calories: 363
Fat: 15.4g

Protein: 42g
Carbohydrates: 10.9g

FENNEL WILD RICE RISOTTO

Time: 35 minutes

Servings: 6

Ingredients:

2 tablespoons extra virgin olive oil
1 shallot, chopped
2 garlic cloves, minced
1 fennel bulb, chopped
1 cup wild rice

¼ cup dry white wine
2 cups chicken stock
1 teaspoon grated orange zest
Salt and pepper to taste

Directions:

Heat the oil in a heavy saucepan.
Add the shallot, garlic and fennel and cook for a few minutes until softened.
Stir in the rice and cook for 2 additional minutes then add the wine, stock and orange zest, as well as salt
    and pepper to taste.
Cook on low heat for 20 minutes.
Serve the risotto warm and fresh.

Nutritional information per serving

Calories: 162

Fat: 5.2g

Protein: 4.8g

Carbohydrates: 24.0g

WILD RICE PRAWN SALAD

Time: 35 minutes

Servings: 6

Ingredients:

¾ cup wild rice
1¾ cups chicken stock
1 pound prawns
Salt and pepper to taste

2 tablespoons lemon juice
2 tablespoons extra virgin olive oil
2 cups arugula

Directions:

Combine the rice and stock in a saucepan and cook until the liquid has been absorbed entirely.
Transfer the rice in a salad bowl.
Season the prawns with salt and pepper and drizzle them with lemon juice and oil.
Heat a grill pan over medium flame.
Place the prawns on the hot pan and cook on each side for 2-3 minutes.
For the salad, combine the rice with arugula and prawns and mix well.
Serve the salad fresh.

Nutritional information per serving

Calories: 207

Fat: 6.4g

Protein: 20.6g

Carbohydrates: 16.7g

CHICKEN BROCCOLI SALAD WITH AVOCADO DRESSING

Time: 40 minutes

Servings: 6

Ingredients:

2 chicken breasts
1 pound broccoli, cut into florets
1 avocado, peeled and pitted
½ lemon, juiced

2 garlic cloves
¼ teaspoon chili powder
¼ teaspoon cumin powder
Salt and pepper to taste

Directions:

Cook the chicken in a large pot of salty water.
Drain and cut the chicken into small cubes. Place in a salad bowl.
Add the broccoli and mix well.
Combine the avocado, lemon juice, garlic, chili powder, cumin powder, salt and pepper in a blender.
    Pulse until smooth.

Spoon the dressing over the salad and mix well.
Serve the salad fresh.

Nutritional information per serving

Calories: 195

Fat: 11g

Protein: 16.4g

Carbohydrates: 9.3g

Seafood Paella

Time: 45 minutes

Servings: 8

Ingredients:

2 tablespoons extra virgin olive oil
1 shallot, chopped
2 garlic cloves, chopped
1 red bell pepper, cored and diced
1 carrot, diced
2 tomatoes, peeled and diced
½ pound fresh shrimps, peeled and deveined
½ pound prawns
1 thyme sprig

1 cup wild rice
1 cup tomato juice
2 cups chicken stock
1 chicken breast, cubed
Salt and pepper to taste
2 monkfish fillets, cubed

1 rosemary sprig

Directions:

Heat the oil in a skillet and stir in the shallot, garlic, bell pepper, carrot and tomatoes. Cook for a few minutes until softened.

Stir in the rice, tomato juice, stock, chicken, salt and pepper and cook on low heat for 20 minutes.

Add the rest of the ingredients and cook for 10 additional minutes.

Serve the paella warm and fresh.

Nutritional information per serving

Calories: 245

Fat: 5.8g

Protein: 27.7g

Carbohydrates: 20.6g

Herbed Roasted Chicken Breasts

Time: 50 minutes

Servings: 4

Ingredients:

2 tablespoons extra virgin olive oil
2 tablespoons chopped parsley
2 tablespoons chopped cilantro
1 teaspoon dried oregano
1 teaspoon dried basil

2 tablespoons lemon juice
Salt and pepper to taste
4 chicken breasts

Directions:

Combine the oil, parsley, cilantro, oregano, basil, lemon juice, salt and pepper in a bowl.

Spread this mixture over the chicken and rub it well into the meat.

Place in a deep dish baking pan and cover with aluminum foil.

Cook in the preheated oven at 350F for 20 minutes then remove the foil and cook for 25 additional minutes.

Serve the chicken warm and fresh with your favorite side dish.

Nutritional information per serving

Calories: 330
Fat: 17.5g

Protein: 40.7g
Carbohydrates: 1g

MARINATED CHICKEN BREASTS

Time: 2 hours

Servings: 4

Ingredients:

4 chicken breasts
Salt and pepper to taste
1 lemon, juiced
1 rosemary sprig
1 thyme sprig

2 garlic cloves, crushed
2 sage leaves
3 tablespoons extra virgin olive oil
½ cup buttermilk

Directions:

Season the chicken with salt and pepper and place it in a zip lock bag.

Add the rest of the ingredients and seal the bag.

Place in the fridge for at least 1 hour.

After 1 hour, heat a grill pan over medium flame then place the chicken on the grill.

Cook on each side for 8-10 minutes or until the juices run out clean.

Serve the chicken warm with your favorite side dish.

Nutritional information per serving

Calories: 371
Fat: 21.1g

Protein: 41.6g
Carbohydrates: 2g

CHICKEN STUFFED BELL PEPPERS

Time: 1½ hours

Servings: 8

Ingredients:

2 pounds ground chicken
2 shallots, chopped
2 garlic cloves, minced
2 tablespoons chopped parsley

½ cup wild rice
1 cup canned chickpeas, drained
1 chili pepper, chopped
Salt and pepper to taste

8 red bell peppers, cored
2 cups diced tomatoes
1 cup chicken stock

1 bay leaf
1 thyme sprig

Directions:

Mix the chicken, shallots, garlic, parsley, wild rice, chickpeas, chili pepper, salt and pepper in a bowl.
Stuff each bell pepper with the chickpea mixture then place them all in a deep dish baking pan.
Pour in the tomatoes and stock and add the bay leaf and thyme.
Cover the pan with aluminum foil and cook in the preheated oven at 350F for 1 hour.
Serve the peppers warm and fresh.

Nutritional information per serving

Calories: 392
Fat: 10.5g

Protein: 40.9g
Carbohydrates: 32.5g

CREAMY TOMATO RISOTTO

Time: 40 minutes

Servings: 4

Ingredients:

2 tablespoons extra virgin olive oil
1 shallot, chopped
1 garlic clove, chopped
3 tomatoes, peeled and diced
⅔ cup wild rice
1½ cups chicken stock
1 rosemary sprig
1 thyme sprig
Salt and pepper to taste

Directions:

Heat the oil in a heavy saucepan.
Add the shallot and garlic and cook for 30 seconds then stir in the tomatoes and rice, as well as stock, rosemary and thyme.
Season with salt and pepper and cook on low heat for 25 minutes.
Serve the risotto warm and fresh.

Nutritional information per serving

Calories: 178
Fat: 7.7g

Protein: 5.1g
Carbohydrates: 24.5g

Spicy Beef Steak with Roasted Bell Pepper Salad

Time: 35 minutes

Servings: 2

Ingredients:

2 beef steaks
1 teaspoon smoked paprika
¼ teaspoon chili powder
½ teaspoon cumin powder

Salt and pepper to taste
6 roasted red bell peppers, chopped
2 tablespoons chopped parsley
1 tablespoon balsamic vinegar

Directions:

Season the beef with paprika, chili powder, cumin powder, salt and pepper.

Heat a grill pan over medium to high heat flame. Place the steaks on the grill and cook on each side for 6-7 minutes.

For the salad, mix the bell peppers, parsley and vinegar in a bowl. Add salt and pepper to taste.

Serve the steaks with pepper salad.

Nutritional information per serving

Calories: 278
Fat: 6.7g

Protein: 29.7g
Carbohydrates: 22.9g

BBQ Prawn Salad

Time: 30 minutes

Servings: 4

Ingredients:

1½ pounds prawns
1 cup BBQ sauce
1 lime, juiced
½ teaspoon chili powder
½ teaspoon cumin powder
2 tablespoons lemon juice
2 tablespoons extra virgin olive oil

2 garlic cloves, minced
Salt and pepper to taste
2 cups arugula
1 mango, peeled and diced
1 red onion, sliced
1 avocado, peeled and sliced
2 tablespoons lemon juice

Directions:

Combine the prawns, BBQ sauce, lime juice, chili powder, cumin powder, lemon juice and oil, as well as garlic, salt and pepper.

Heat a grill pan over medium flame and place the prawns on the grill.

Cook on each side for 2 minutes.

Combine the arugula, prawns, mango, red onion, avocado and lemon juice in a salad bowl and mix well.

Serve the salad fresh.

Nutritional information per serving

Calories: 347
Fat: 13.6g

Protein: 27.3g
Carbohydrates: 29.5g

ROASTED SEA BASS

Time: 35 minutes
Servings: 6

Ingredients:

6 sea bass fillets
Salt and pepper to taste
1 chili, chopped
½ teaspoon cumin powder

2 tablespoons extra virgin olive oil
2 tablespoons lemon juice
1 rosemary sprig
1 pound potatoes, peeled

Directions:

Season the sea bass with salt and pepper.
Combine the chili, cumin powder, oil, lemon juice, rosemary sprig and potatoes in a deep dish baking pan.
Place the sea bass on top and seal the pan with aluminum foil.
Cook in the preheated oven at 350F for 30 minutes.
Serve the dish warm.

Nutritional information per serving

Calories: 267
Fat: 9.8g

Protein: 27.7g
Carbohydrates: 17.2g

SPICED CHICKEN CAULIFLOWER SALAD

Time: 40 minutes
Servings: 6

Ingredients:

1 large cauliflower head, cut into florets
2 chicken breasts, cooked and cubed
1 celery stalk, sliced
1 green onion, sliced
1 teaspoon curry powder

½ teaspoon chili powder
½ teaspoon cumin powder
1 avocado, peeled and pitted
1 lime, juiced
Salt and pepper to taste

Directions:

Combine the cauliflower, chicken, celery and green onion in a salad bowl.
Combine the curry powder, chili powder, cumin, avocado and lime juice in a blender. Add salt and pepper and pulse until smooth.
Spoon the dressing over the salad and mix well.
Serve it fresh.

Nutritional information per serving

Calories: 187
Fat: 10.2g

Protein: 15.6g
Carbohydrates: 7.1g

ASIAN STYLE POACHED SEA BASS

Time: 25 minutes   Servings: 4

Ingredients:

1 teaspoon grated ginger
2 garlic cloves, sliced
1 tablespoon soy sauce
1 teaspoon black peppercorns

1 teaspoon sesame oil
2 cups vegetable stock
4 sea bass fillets

Directions:

Combine the ginger, garlic, soy sauce, peppercorns and sesame oil in a pot. Add the stock as well and
    bring to a boil.
Place the fish in the pot and cover with a lid.
Cook for 7-8 minutes then carefully remove the fish and serve it fresh with your favorite side dish.

Nutritional information per serving

Calories: 146   Protein: 24.5g
Fat: 3.8g   Carbohydrates: 1.9g

GRILLED SALMON WITH CREAMED SPINACH

Time: 45 minutes   Servings: 4

Ingredients:

2 salmon fillets
Salt and pepper to taste
1 teaspoon dried basil
1 teaspoon dried oregano
2 tablespoons extra virgin olive oil

2 garlic cloves, minced
1 pound spinach, shredded
1 red chili, chopped
½ cup cream cheese

Directions:

Season the salmon with salt, pepper, basil and oregano.
Heat a grill pan over medium flame then place the fish on the grill.
Cook on each side for 4-5 minutes.
For the spinach, heat the oil in a skillet and add the garlic. Cook for 30 seconds then add the spinach.
Cook for 10 minutes until most of the liquid is reduced.
Add the red chili and cream cheese and mix well. Cook for 5 additional minutes.
Serve the fish with the spinach warm.

Nutritional information per serving

Calories: 309   Protein: 22.9g
Fat: 23.1g   Carbohydrates: 5.7g

Root Vegetable Lentil Stew

Time: 45 minutes

Servings: 8

Ingredients:

2 tablespoons extra virgin olive oil
2 shallots, sliced
4 garlic cloves, chopped
2 carrots, sliced
2 parsnips, sliced
2 turnips, peeled and diced
1 jalapeño pepper, chopped
1 cup green lentils

½ teaspoon chili powder
1 teaspoon cumin powder
½ teaspoon garam masala
1 bay leaf
1 cup diced tomatoes
2 cups vegetable stock
Salt and pepper to taste

Directions:

Heat the oil in a heavy saucepan and add the shallots and garlic. cook for 2 minutes then stir in the rest of the ingredients.

Season with salt and pepper then cook the stew on low heat for 30 minutes.

Serve the stew warm and fresh.

Nutritional information per serving

Calories: 166
Fat: 4.0g

Protein: 7.5g
Carbohydrates: 26.3g

Green Salmon Burgers

Time: 40 minutes

Servings: 4

Ingredients:

4 salmon fillets
4 garlic cloves, minced
2 tablespoons chopped dill
1 tablespoon chopped parsley

4 garlic cloves, minced
1 tablespoon green curry paste
Salt and pepper to taste

Directions:

Place the salmon in a food processor and pulse until well mixed and ground.

Add the rest of the ingredients and season with salt and pepper.

Form 4 burgers.

Heat a grill pan over medium flame. Place the burgers on the grill and cook for 3-4 minutes on each side.

Serve the burgers warm with your favorite toppings.

Nutritional information per serving

Calories: 260
Fat: 11.9g

Protein: 35.2g
Carbohydrates: 4.1g

PRAWN TOMATO STEW

Time: 45 minutes   Servings: 6

Ingredients:

2 tablespoons extra virgin olive oil
1 shallot, sliced
2 garlic cloves, chopped
2 celery stalks, sliced
2 carrots, sliced
1 pound potatoes, peeled and cubed

1½ cups diced tomatoes
1 bay leaf
1 thyme sprig
Salt and pepper to taste
1½ cups vegetable stock
1 pound prawns

Directions:

Heat the oil in skillet and stir in the shallot and garlic, as well as celery and carrots.
Cook for a few minutes until softened, then add the potatoes, tomatoes, bay leaf and thyme, as well as salt and pepper to taste.
Pour in the stock and cook on low heat for 20 minutes.
Add the prawns and cook for 10 additional minutes.
Serve the stew warm.

Nutritional information per serving

Calories: 203   Protein: 19.2g
Fat: 6.3g   Carbohydrates: 17.7g

WILD MUSHROOM RISOTTO

Time: 30 minutes   Servings: 6

Ingredients:

2 tablespoons extra virgin olive oil
1 shallot, chopped
1 garlic clove, chopped
1 cup wild rice
2 oz. wild mushrooms, chopped

½ pound champignon mushrooms, sliced
¼ cup dry white wine
2 cups chicken stock
2 tablespoons cream cheese
Salt and pepper to taste

Directions:

Heat the oil in a heavy saucepan. Add the shallot and garlic and cook for 30 seconds then stir in the rest of the ingredients.
Season with salt and pepper and cook on low heat for 20 minutes.
Serve the dish warm and fresh.

Nutritional information per serving

Calories: 170   Protein: 6.0g
Fat: 6.5g   Carbohydrates: 22.6g

Spanish Meatball Stew

Time: 45 minutes

Servings: 8

Ingredients:

2 pounds ground beef
4 garlic cloves, minced
1 shallot, chopped
2 tablespoons chopped parsley
½ teaspoon chili powder
½ teaspoon cumin powder

1 can diced tomatoes
½ cup dry white wine
1 cup chicken stock
1 bay leaf
1 thyme sprig
Salt and pepper to taste

Directions:

Combine the ground beef, garlic, shallot, parsley, chili and cumin powder in a bowl. Mix well then form small meatballs and place them on a chopping board.

Combine the tomatoes, wine, stock, bay leaf and thyme in a saucepan.

Bring to a boil then add the meatballs.

Cover the pot and cook on low heat for 30 minutes. Add salt and pepper to taste.

Serve the stew warm and fresh.

Nutritional information per serving

Calories: 231
Fat: 7.2g

Protein: 34.8g
Carbohydrates: 1.9g

Spicy Roasted Vegetables

Time: 45 minutes

Servings: 6

Ingredients:

1 zucchini, sliced
1 parsnip, sliced
1 turnip, cubed
2 carrots, sliced
2 red bell peppers, cored and sliced
2 yellow bell peppers, cored and sliced
4 garlic cloves, chopped

2 red onions, sliced
2 cups cherry tomatoes
1 teaspoon cumin powder
1½ teaspoons chili powder
2 tablespoons extra virgin olive oil
Salt and pepper to taste

Directions:

Combine all the ingredients in a deep dish baking pan.

Season with salt and pepper and cook in the preheated oven at 350F for 30 minutes.

Serve the dish warm and fresh.

Nutritional information per serving

Calories: 132
Fat: 5.4g

Protein: 3.0g
Carbohydrates: 20.1g

Squash Gorgonzola Pilaf

Time: 50 minutes   Servings: 6

Ingredients:

2 tablespoons extra virgin olive oil
1 shallot, chopped
2 garlic cloves, chopped
2 cups butternut squash cubes
1 teaspoon cumin seeds

1 cup wild rice
½ teaspoon dried sage
2 cups chicken stock
Salt and pepper to taste
2 oz. gorgonzola, crumbled

Directions:

Heat the oil in a skillet.
Add the shallot and garlic and cook for 30 seconds then add the butternut squash, cumin seeds and rice, as well as sage.
Cook for 5 additional minutes then pour in the stock and season with salt and pepper.
Cook on low heat for 20-25 minutes then top with gorgonzola.
Serve the dish warm.

Nutritional information per serving

Calories: 189
Fat: 7.9g

Protein: 6.7g
Carbohydrates: 24.9g

Minty Eggplant Salad

Time: 25 minutes   Servings: 4

Ingredients:

2 large eggplants, cut into slices
Salt and pepper to taste
2 tablespoons extra virgin olive oil
1 teaspoon dried basil

1 teaspoon dried oregano
1 teaspoon dried mint
2 tablespoons balsamic vinegar

Directions:

Season the eggplant slices with salt and pepper.
Heat a grill pan over medium flame and place the eggplant on the grill. Cook on each side for a few minutes until browned.
When done, transfer the eggplant in a bowl and add the rest of the ingredients.
Mix well and serve the salad fresh.

Nutritional information per serving

Calories: 132
Fat: 7.5g

Protein: 2.8g
Carbohydrates: 16.5g

EGGPLANT COUSCOUS

Time: 35 minutes

Servings: 6

Ingredients:

2 small eggplants, sliced
Salt and pepper to taste
½ cup couscous
1½ cups vegetable stock, hot
1 cup chopped parsley

¼ cup chopped cilantro
1 cup cherry tomatoes, quartered
¼ cup pomegranate seeds
2 tablespoons extra virgin olive oil
1 lemon, juiced

Directions:

Season the eggplants with salt and pepper.

Heat a grill pan over medium flame. Place the eggplant on the grill and cook on each side for 2-3 minutes until browned.

While the eggplant cooks, combine the couscous and stock in a bowl. Cover with a lid and allow to soak up the liquid for 15 minutes. When done, fluff it up with a fork.

Add the eggplant and the rest of the ingredients. Season with salt and pepper and mix well.

Serve the couscous fresh.

Nutritional information per serving

Calories: 153
Fat: 5.4g

Protein: 4.3g
Carbohydrates: 24.8g

SPICED TURKEY PATTIES IN TOMATO SAUCE

Time: 50 minutes

Servings: 8

Ingredients:

1 can diced tomatoes
1½ cups chicken stock
1 bay leaf
2 tablespoons tomato paste
2 pounds ground turkey
1 carrot, grated
½ teaspoon chili powder

½ teaspoon cumin powder
½ teaspoon dried oregano
1 red onion, chopped
6 garlic cloves, minced
1 teaspoon ground coriander
Salt and pepper to taste

Directions:

Combine the tomatoes, stock, bay leaf and tomato paste in a deep dish baking pan.

For the patties, mix the turkey, carrot, spices, onion and garlic in a bowl. Add salt and pepper to taste and mix well.

Form small patties and place them in the tomato sauce.

Cover with aluminum foil and cook in the preheated oven at 350F for 35 minutes.

Serve the patties and sauce warm.

Nutritional information per serving

Calories: 255
Fat: 12.7g

Protein: 31.7g
Carbohydrates: 3.9g

 Sweet Potato Lentil Curry

Time: 50 minutes

Servings: 6

Ingredients:

2 tablespoons extra virgin olive oil
2 shallots, chopped
2 garlic cloves, minced
½ teaspoon ground coriander
½ teaspoon cumin powder
¼ teaspoon chili powder
1 teaspoon curry powder
4 sweet potatoes, peeled and cubed

¼ cup red lentils
2 cups vegetable stock
1 cup diced tomatoes
2 kaffir lime leaves
1 bay leaf
1 thyme sprig
Salt and pepper to taste

Directions:

Heat the oil in a heavy saucepan and add the shallots and garlic. Cook for 1 minute then add the spices and cook for 30 seconds until fragrant.
Stir in the sweet potatoes, red lentils, stock, tomatoes, kaffir lime leaves, bay leaf and thyme.
Adjust the taste with salt and pepper and cook on low heat for 30 minutes.
Serve the curry fresh and warm.

Nutritional information per serving

Calories: 203
Fat: 5.1g

Protein: 4.2g
Carbohydrates: 36.4g

One Pan Roasted Pork Chops with Spiced Butternut Squash

Time: 1¼ hours

Servings: 6

Ingredients:

6 pork chops
4 cups butternut squash cubes
Salt and pepper to taste
½ teaspoon chili powder

½ teaspoon cumin powder
½ teaspoon ground coriander
2 tablespoons balsamic vinegar
2 tablespoons extra virgin olive oil

Directions:

Season the pork chops and butternut squash with salt and pepper.
Sprinkle the butternut squash with spices and place them in a deep dish baking pan.
Drizzle with vinegar and olive oil and place the pork chops on top.

Bake in the preheated oven at 350F for 45 minutes.
Serve the pork chops and squash warm.

Nutritional information per serving

Calories: 325
Fat: 24.6g

Protein: 18.7g
Carbohydrates: 6.9g

QUINOA COD PILAF

Time: 35 minutes

Servings: 4

Ingredients:

2 tablespoons extra virgin olive oil
1 shallot, chopped
2 garlic cloves, minced
½ cup quinoa, rinsed

1½ cups vegetable stock
2 cups broccoli florets
4 cod fillets, cubed
Salt and pepper to taste

Directions:

Heat the oil in a skillet and stir in the shallot and garlic. Cook for 1 minute then add the quinoa and stock.
Stir in the broccoli florets and cod fillets and adjust the taste with salt and pepper.
Cook on low heat for 20 minutes.
Serve the pilaf warm.

Nutritional information per serving

Calories: 239
Fat: 8.9g

Protein: 23.4g
Carbohydrates: 17.8g

CHICKEN WHITE BEAN CASSEROLE

Time: 1 hour

Servings: 8

Ingredients:

1 can white beans, drained
2 zucchinis, cubed
2 red bell peppers, cored and sliced
1 shallot, sliced
2 tomatoes, diced

1 bay leaf
1 teaspoon dried basil
1 cup chicken stock
Salt and pepper to taste
4 chicken breasts, halved

Directions:

Combine the white beans, zucchinis, bell peppers, shallot, tomatoes, bay leaf, basil and stock in a deep dish baking pan.
Add salt and pepper to taste.
Season the chicken with salt and pepper as well and place the chicken over the beans.

Cover with aluminum foil and cook in the preheated oven at 350F for 30 minutes then remove the foil and cook for another 15 minutes.

Serve the chicken and vegetables warm.

Nutritional information per serving

Calories: 244

Fat: 5.7g

Protein: 27.4g

Carbohydrates: 19.9g

SPICED LAMB CHOPS WITH CHICKPEA SAUTÉ

Time: 1 hour

Servings: 6

Ingredients:

6 lamb chops
Salt and pepper to taste
1 can chickpeas, drained
4 carrots, sliced
1 teaspoon dried oregano
1 cup diced tomatoes

1 bay leaf
1 cup chicken stock
½ teaspoon chili powder
½ teaspoon cumin powder
½ teaspoon ground coriander
½ teaspoon dried basil

Directions:

Season the lamb chops with salt and pepper.

Combine the chickpeas, carrots, oregano, tomatoes, bay leaf, stock and spices in a deep dish baking pan.

Place the lamb chops over the vegetables and bake in the preheated oven at 350F for 35 minutes.

Serve the chops and veggies warm.

Nutritional information per serving

Calories: 305

Fat: 8.5g

Protein: 31.1g

Carbohydrates: 25.9g

SEARED SALMON WITH TROPICAL WATERCRESS SALAD

Time: 30 minutes

Servings: 6

Ingredients:

4 salmon fillets
Salt and pepper to taste
1 teaspoon dried thyme
4 watercress, trimmed
1 mango, peeled and diced

1 papaya, peeled and diced
1 lime, juiced
2 tablespoons extra virgin olive oil
Salt and pepper to taste

Directions:

Season the salmon with salt, pepper and thyme.

Heat a grill pan over medium flame then place the salmon on the grill. Cook on each side for 3-4 minutes until golden.

For the salad, combine the remaining ingredients in a bowl. Adjust the taste with salt and pepper.

Serve the salmon with the fresh salad.

Nutritional information per serving

Calories: 259
Fat: 12.3g

Protein: 24.2g
Carbohydrates: 13.5g

ORANGE FLAVORED CHICKEN

Time: 45 minutes

Servings: 4

Ingredients:

4 chicken breasts
Salt and pepper to taste
2 tablespoons all-purpose flour
2 tablespoons extra virgin olive oil
2 shallots, sliced
2 garlic cloves, minced

2 oranges, cut into segments
1 star anise
½ cinnamon stick
1 red chili, sliced
1 cup chicken stock

Directions:

Season the chicken with salt and pepper then sprinkle it with flour.

Heat the oil in a saucepan. Add the chicken and cook on each side until golden brown.

Add the shallots and garlic and cook for 1 minute until softened.

Stir in the rest of the ingredients and season with salt and pepper.

Cook on low heat for 25 minutes until reduced and the chicken has clean juices.

Serve the chicken warm.

Nutritional information per serving

Calories: 388
Fat: 17.7g

Protein: 42g
Carbohydrates: 14.5g

CHICKEN BULGUR PILAF

Time: 45 minutes

Servings: 4

Ingredients:

2 tablespoons extra virgin olive oil
1 shallot, chopped
2 chicken breasts, cubed
1 carrot, diced
1 celery stalk, diced
1 shallot, chopped

1 red bell pepper, cored and diced
1 yellow bell pepper, cored and diced
1 cup diced tomatoes
½ cup bulgur
1½ cups chicken stock
Salt and pepper to taste

Directions:

Heat the oil in a heavy saucepan and stir in the shallot and chicken. Cook for a few minutes on all sides.
Add the rest of the ingredients and season with salt and pepper.
Cook on low heat for 30 minutes.
Serve the pilaf warm and fresh.

Nutritional information per serving

Calories: 294

Fat: 12.9g

Protein: 23.9g

Carbohydrates: 21.4g

Chicken Saltimbocca

Time: 30 minutes

Servings: 4

Ingredients:

4 chicken fillets
Salt and pepper to taste
2 tablespoons all-purpose flour
4 prosciutto slices
4 sage leaves

2 tablespoons extra virgin olive oil
¼ cup dry Marsala wine
½ cup chicken stock
½ cup tomato juice

Directions:

Season the chicken with salt and pepper and sprinkle it with flour.
Wrap each fillet in prosciutto and seal it with a toothpick, placing a sage leaf on top as well.
Heat the oil in a skillet and add the chicken in the hot oil. Cook on each side until golden brown, for 3-4 minutes.
Add the rest of the ingredients and cook on low heat for 20 minutes.
Serve the saltimbocca warm.

Nutritional information per serving

Calories: 369

Fat: 17.9g

Protein: 41.5g

Carbohydrates: 5.7g

Herb Stuffed Chicken Thighs

Time: 45 minutes

Servings: 4

Ingredients:

¼ cup chopped cilantro
¼ cup chopped parsley
3 tablespoons extra virgin olive oil
½ teaspoon paprika
1 teaspoon salt

½ teaspoon dried oregano
4 chicken thighs
1 cup chicken stock

Directions:

Mix the cilantro, parsley, oil, paprika, salt and oregano in a bowl.

Spread this mixture over the chicken thighs and place them all in a deep dish baking pan.

Pour in the stock and cover with aluminum foil.

Cook in the preheated oven at 350F for 30 minutes then remove the foil and cook for 10 additional minutes.

Serve the chicken thighs warm with your favorite side dish.

Nutritional information per serving

Calories: 362
Fat: 21.1g

Protein: 40.9g
Carbohydrates: 0.7g

CHIMICHURRI SALMON

Time: 35 minutes

Servings: 4

Ingredients:

4 salmon fillets
Salt and pepper to taste
1½ cups chopped parsley
6 garlic cloves

2 tablespoons pine nuts
3 tablespoons extra virgin olive oil
¼ teaspoon red pepper flakes
2 tablespoons lemon juice

Directions:

Season the salmon with salt and pepper.

Heat a grill pan over medium flame then place the fish on the grill. Cook on each side for 4-5 minutes.

For the sauce, combine the parsley, garlic, pine nuts, oil, red pepper flakes and lemon juice in a blender and pulse until smooth.

Serve the salmon drizzled with parsley sauce.

Serve the fish right away.

Nutritional information per serving

Calories: 371
Fat: 24.7g

Protein: 36.2g
Carbohydrates: 3.7g

BEET FETA SALAD

Time: 15 minutes

Servings: 2

Ingredients:

2 large red beets, cooked and cubed
2 cups arugula
4 oz. feta cheese, cubed
1 tablespoon balsamic vinegar

1 pinch chili powder

Directions:

Combine the beets, arugula, feta cheese, vinegar and chili powder in a salad bowl.
Mix gently and serve the salad right away.

Nutritional information per serving

Calories: 232
Fat: 12.5g

Protein: 11.5g
Carbohydrates: 20.1g

Chicken Snow Pea Stir-Fry

Time: 25 minutes

Servings: 4

Ingredients:

2 tablespoons extra virgin olive oil
2 garlic cloves, minced
1 shallot, sliced
1 teaspoon grated ginger
½ teaspoon cumin seeds

½ teaspoon ground coriander
2 chicken breasts, cut into thin strips
1 pound snow peas
1 tablespoon soy sauce
1 teaspoon sesame oil

Directions:

Heat the oil in a skillet. Stir in the garlic and shallot and cook for 1 minute until softened.
Stir in the ginger, cumin seeds, coriander and chicken and cook on high heat for 10 minutes.
Add the snow peas and cook for 5 additional minutes.
Stir in the soy sauce and sesame oil.
Serve right away.

Nutritional information per serving

Calories: 259
Fat: 13.7g

Protein: 24.5g
Carbohydrates: 9.7g

Pasta Primavera

Time: 30 minutes

Servings: 6

Ingredients:

12 oz. spaghetti
2 tablespoons extra virgin olive oil
1 garlic clove, chopped
½ teaspoon grated ginger
1 shallot, sliced
2 cups broccoli florets
1 cup green peas
1 cup snow peas

Salt and pepper to taste

Directions:

Pour a few cups of water in a large pot and add a pinch of salt. Throw in the pasta and cook for 8 minutes then drain well.

Heat the oil in a skillet and stir in the garlic and ginger. Cook for 30 seconds then add the shallot, broccoli, green peas and snow peas.

Add salt and pepper to taste and cook for 10 minutes.

Stir in the spaghetti and mix well.

Serve the pasta fresh.

Nutritional information per serving

Calories: 247
Fat: 6.2g

Protein: 9.5g
Carbohydrates: 39.0g

EDAMAME STEW

Time: 45 minutes

Servings: 4

Ingredients:

2 tablespoons extra virgin olive oil
1 sweet onion, chopped
2 garlic cloves, minced
1 zucchini, sliced
½ teaspoon cumin powder
½ teaspoon ground coriander

1 pinch chili flakes
16 oz. frozen edamame
1 cup diced tomatoes
1 cup vegetable stock
1 bay leaf
Salt and pepper to taste

Directions:

Heat the oil in a heavy saucepan. Add the onion and garlic and cook for 1 minute.

Stir in the rest of the ingredients and season with salt and pepper.

Cook on low heat for 25 minutes.

Serve the stew warm and fresh.

Nutritional information per serving

Calories: 273
Fat: 14.9g

Protein: 21.2g
Carbohydrates: 21.9g

SWORDFISH TOMATO STEW

Time: 35 minutes

Servings: 4

Ingredients:

1 can diced tomatoes
½ cup dry white wine
½ cup chicken stock
1 bay leaf

1 thyme sprig
1 rosemary sprig
4 swordfish fillets
Salt and pepper to taste

Directions:

Combine the tomatoes, wine, stock, bay leaf, thyme and rosemary in a deep dish baking pan.
Season the fish with salt and pepper and place it in the tomato mixture.
Cover with aluminum foil and cook in the preheated oven at 350F for 25 minutes.
Serve the stew warm and fresh.

Nutritional information per serving

Calories: 208

Protein: 27.4g

Fat: 5.6g

Carbohydrates: 2.7g

Dijon Roasted Chicken

Time: 2 hours

Servings: 8

Ingredients:

3 tablespoons Dijon mustard
2 tablespoons extra virgin olive oil
1 teaspoon dried dill
1 teaspoon dried basil

1 teaspoon dried oregano
Salt and pepper to taste
1 whole chicken
1 cup dry white wine

Directions:

Mix the mustard, oil, dill, basil and oregano in a bowl. Add salt and pepper to taste.
Spread this mixture over the chicken, rubbing it well into the skin.
Place the chicken in a deep dish baking pan.
Pour in the wine and cover the pan with a sheet of aluminum foil.
Bake in the preheated oven at 350F for 1¼ hours then remove the foil and cook for 30 additional minutes.
Serve the chicken warm with your favorite side dish.

Nutritional information per serving

Calories: 325

Protein: 40.8g

Fat: 14.1g

Carbohydrates: 1.3g

Za'atar Roasted Chicken Breast

Time: 1 hour

Servings: 4

Ingredients:

4 chicken breasts
Salt and pepper to taste
2 tablespoons za'atar

3 tablespoons extra virgin olive oil
½ lemon, juiced
½ orange, juiced

Directions:

Season the chicken with salt, pepper and za'atar and place it in a deep dish baking pan.

Drizzle with olive oil, lemon juice and orange juice.

Cook in the preheated oven at 350F for 35-40 minutes.

Serve the chicken warm with your favorite side dish.

Nutritional information per serving

Calories: 367

Fat: 20.9g

Protein: 40.7g

Carbohydrates: 2.7g

ORANGE STUFFED ROASTED CHICKEN

Time: 2 hours

Servings: 8

Ingredients:

1 whole chicken

Salt and pepper to taste

2 tablespoons Cajun seasoning

2 oranges, halved

2 rosemary sprigs

2 tablespoons extra virgin olive oil

Directions:

Season the chicken with salt, pepper and Cajun seasoning.

Place the chicken in a deep dish baking pan.

Stuff the chicken with the oranges and rosemary and drizzle the chicken with olive oil.

Cover with aluminum foil and cook in the preheated oven at 350F for 1 hour then remove the foil and cook for additional 40 minutes.

Serve the chicken warm with your favorite side dish.

Nutritional information per serving

Calories: 318

Fat: 13.9g

Protein: 41g

Carbohydrates: 5.4g

VEGGIE RED CURRY

Time: 50 minutes

Servings: 8

Ingredients:

2 tablespoons extra virgin olive oil

1 shallot, chopped

4 garlic cloves, minced

2 red bell peppers, cored and diced

2 carrots, diced

1 turnip, peeled and cubed

1 parsnip, diced

2 sweet potatoes, peeled and cubed

1 zucchini, cubed

½ pound snow peas

1 cup diced tomatoes

4 tablespoons red curry paste

¼ teaspoon chili powder

½ teaspoon cumin powder

½ teaspoon ground coriander

1 bay leaf

1 cup vegetable stock

Salt and pepper to taste

Chopped cilantro for serving

Directions:

Heat the oil in a saucepan and add the shallot, garlic, bell pepper and carrots. Cook for 5 minutes until softened.

Stir in the turnip and the rest of the vegetables, as well as the curry paste, spices, bay leaf and stock.

Adjust the taste with salt and pepper and cover the pot with a lid.

Cook on low heat for 30 minutes.

Serve the curry warm, sprinkled with freshly chopped cilantro.

Nutritional information per serving

Calories: 161
Fat: 6.2g

Protein: 3.0g
Carbohydrates: 23.9g

CREAMY LEMON SEARED COD

Time: 25 minutes

Servings: 4

Ingredients:

4 cod fillets
Salt and pepper to taste
2 tablespoons extra virgin olive oil
2 garlic cloves, minced

1 lemon, sliced
¼ cup vegetable stock
½ cup heavy cream

Directions:

Season the cod with salt and pepper.

Heat the oil in a skillet and add the cod.

Cook for 2 minutes on high heat until browned on each side.

Stir in the garlic, lemon and stock and cook for 5 minutes.

Remove the lemon slices and stir in the cream.

Remove from heat and serve right away.

Nutritional information per serving

Calories: 204
Fat: 13g

Protein: 20.5g
Carbohydrates: 0.9g

BEEF MUSHROOM STIR-FRY

Time: 25 minutes

Servings: 4

Ingredients:

2 tablespoons peanut oil
1 pound beef flank steak, cut into strips
2 garlic cloves, minced
1 teaspoon grated ginger

4 Portobello mushrooms, sliced
1 tablespoon soy sauce
1 tablespoon lemon juice
1 teaspoon sesame oil

1 teaspoon rice vinegar

2 green onions, chopped

Directions:

Heat the peanut oil in a skillet or wok and stir in the beef.

Cook on high heat for 5 minutes then add the garlic, ginger and mushrooms.

Cook for another 5 minutes on high heat, stirring often.

Add the soy sauce, lemon juice, sesame oil and vinegar and cook for another 5 minutes.

Remove from heat and serve right away, sprinkled with green onions.

Nutritional information per serving

Calories: 310
Fat: 15.0g

Protein: 38.0g
Carbohydrates: 4.8g

QUICK BOK CHOY STIR-FRY

Time: 15 minutes

Servings: 4

Ingredients:

2 tablespoons peanut oil
2 garlic cloves, minced
½ teaspoon grated ginger
1 shallot, sliced
2 red bell peppers, cored and sliced

2 Portobello mushrooms, sliced
2 bok choy, shredded
1 tablespoon soy sauce
1 teaspoon rice vinegar
1 red chili, sliced

Directions:

Heat the oil in a skillet and stir in the garlic, ginger and shallot. Cook for 1 minute on high heat then add the bell peppers and mushrooms.

Cook for 5 minutes then stir in the bok choy and cook for 5 additional minutes.

Add the soy sauce, vinegar and red chili and remove from heat.

Serve the stir-fry right away.

Nutritional information per serving

Calories: 101
Fat: 7.0g

Protein: 3.1g
Carbohydrates: 7.4g

ANCHO HONEY ROASTED SALMON

Time: 25 minutes

Servings: 4

Ingredients:

2 tablespoons raw honey
2 ancho chili peppers, chopped
½ teaspoon onion powder

2 tablespoons lime juice
2 tablespoons soy sauce
4 salmon fillets

Directions:

Mix the honey, chili peppers, onion powder, lime juice and soy sauce in a bowl.
Brush the salmon with this mixture and place the fish in a baking tray.
Bake in the preheated oven at 350F for 10 minutes.
Serve the salmon fresh with your favorite side dish.

Nutritional information per serving

Calories: 364
Fat: 19.6g

Protein: 35.7g
Carbohydrates: 12.9g

BUTTERNUT SQUASH POSOLE

Time: 1 hour

Servings: 8

Ingredients:

4 cups butternut squash cubes
1 can white beans, drained
1 can diced tomatoes
½ teaspoon chili powder
½ teaspoon cumin powder
1 red onion, chopped

1 can sweet corn, drained
1 bay leaf
1½ cups vegetable stock
Salt and pepper to taste
Chopped cilantro for serving

Directions:

Combine all the ingredients in a deep dish baking pan.
Season with salt and pepper and cover the pan with aluminum foil.
Cook in the preheated oven at 350F for 30 minutes.
Serve the posole warm and fresh, topped with chopped cilantro.

Nutritional information per serving

Calories: 129
Fat: 0.5g

Protein: 7.2g
Carbohydrates: 25.9g

ALMOND CRUSTED COD

Time: 25 minutes

Servings: 4

Ingredients:

½ cup almond flour
½ cup sliced almonds
Salt and pepper to taste

4 cod fillets
1 egg, beaten

Directions:

Mix the almond flour, sliced almonds, salt and pepper in a bowl.

Season the cod with salt and pepper then dip each fillet into the beaten egg then roll them through the almond mixture.

Place the fish on a baking tray lined with baking paper and bake in the preheated oven at 350F for 15 minutes.

Serve the cod warm with your favorite side dish.

Nutritional information per serving

Calories: 205
Fat: 9.2g

Protein:24.7g
Carbohydrates: 3.4g

SPICY VEGETABLE NOODLES

Time: 30 minutes

Servings: 6

Ingredients:

12 oz. rice noodles
2 tablespoons coconut oil
2 garlic cloves, minced
1 shallot, sliced
1 zucchini, sliced

1 red bell pepper, cored and sliced
1 teaspoon grated ginger
2 cups snow peas
1 tablespoon soy sauce
1 teaspoon dry sherry

Directions:

Pour a few cups of water in a pot and add the rice noodles. Cook them according to the package instructions then drain well.

Heat the oil in a skillet or frying pan then stir in the garlic and shallot. Cook for 1 minute then stir in the rest of the ingredients and cook for 10 minutes.

Remove from heat and stir in the rice noodles.

Serve the dish warm and fresh.

Nutritional information per serving

Calories: 149
Fat: 4.9g

Protein: 3.2g
Carbohydrates: 21.3g

CHILI RUBBED STEAKS

Time: 20 minutes

Servings: 2

Ingredients:

2 beef steaks
2 tablespoons extra virgin olive oil
1 teaspoon smoked paprika
1 teaspoon chili powder
1 teaspoon salt

Directions:

Drizzle the steaks with olive oil then sprinkle with the spices and salt and rub the meat well.

Heat a grill pan over medium to high heat then place the steaks on the grill.

Cook on each side for 3-4 minutes or more, depending how well done you want them.

Serve the steaks warm with your favorite side dish.

Nutritional information per serving

Calories: 285
Fat: 19.7g

Protein: 26.1g
Carbohydrates: 1.3g

Baked Halibut Steaks

Time: 20 minutes

Servings: 4

Ingredients:

4 halibut steaks
Salt and pepper to taste
1 teaspoon lemon zest
1 tablespoon lemon juice

1 teaspoon dried thyme
1 garlic clove, minced
2 tablespoons extra virgin olive oil
2 cups cherry tomatoes

Directions:

Season the fish with salt and pepper.

In a bowl, mix the lemon zest, lemon juice, thyme, garlic and olive oil.

Brush this mixture over the halibut and place it in a baking tray lined with parchment paper.
Add the tomatoes as well.

Bake in the preheated oven at 350F for 15 minutes.

Serve the steaks warm with your favorite side dish.

Nutritional information per serving

Calories: 331
Fat:12.5g

Protein: 48.6g
Carbohydrates: 4.1g

Maple Glazed Salmon

Time: 25 minutes

Servings: 4

Ingredients:

3 tablespoons maple syrup
1 garlic clove, minced
1 tablespoon soy sauce

2 tablespoons extra virgin olive oil
4 salmon fillets

Directions:

Mix the maple syrup, garlic, soy sauce and oil in a bowl.

Brush the fish with this mixture and place it in a baking tray lined with parchment paper.

Bake in the preheated oven at 350F for 15 minutes.
Serve the salmon warm with your favorite side dish.

Nutritional information per serving

Calories: 338
Fat: 18.0g

Protein: 34.8g
Carbohydrates: 10.6g

BRAISED BALSAMIC CHICKEN

Time: 1 hour

Servings: 4

Ingredients:

4 chicken breasts
Salt and pepper to taste
3 tablespoons balsamic vinegar

2 tablespoons extra virgin olive oil
2 thyme sprigs
1 rosemary sprig

Directions:

Season the chicken with salt and pepper and place it in a deep dish baking pan.
Drizzle the chicken with vinegar and oil then place the herb sprigs on top.
Cover the pan with aluminum foil and bake in the preheated oven at 350F for 30 minutes.
Remove the foil and cook for 10 additional minutes on 400F.
Serve the chicken warm with your favorite side dish.

Nutritional information per serving

Calories: 328
Fat: 17.4g

Protein: 40.5g
Carbohydrates: 0.1g

SPICED COUSCOUS WITH CHICKEN THIGHS

Time: 1 hour

Servings: 6

Ingredients:

1 cup couscous
½ teaspoon cumin powder
½ teaspoon chili powder
1 jalapeño pepper, chopped
1 can chickpeas, drained

1 bay leaf
Salt and pepper to taste
2½ cups chicken stock
6 chicken thighs

Directions:

Mix the couscous, cumin powder, chili powder, pepper, chickpeas and bay leaf in a deep dish baking pan. Add salt and pepper to taste.
Pour in the stock then place the chicken over the couscous and cook in the preheated oven at 350F for 35-40 minutes.
Serve the couscous and chicken warm.

Nutritional information per serving

Calories: 498
Fat: 12.6g

Protein: 50.7g
Carbohydrates: 42g

FIVE-SPICE ROASTED TURKEY AND MUSHROOMS

Time: 1 hour   Servings: 6

Ingredients:

1½ pounds turkey breast
Salt and pepper to taste
1 teaspoon five-spice powder
½ teaspoon chili powder
½ teaspoon cumin powder

4 Portobello mushrooms, sliced
1 rosemary sprig
1 thyme sprig
1 bay leaf
½ cup dry white wine

Directions:

Season the turkey with salt and pepper, as well as five-spice powder, chili and cumin.

Place the turkey in a deep dish baking pan then add the mushrooms, rosemary sprig, thyme and bay leaf, as well as the wine.

Cover the pan with aluminum foil and cook in the preheated oven at 350F for 30 minutes then remove the foil and cook for 20 additional minutes.

Serve the dish warm and fresh.

Nutritional information per serving

Calories: 157
Fat: 2.0g

Protein: 22.0g
Carbohydrates: 8.0g

CHIPOTLE GLAZED CHICKEN

Time: 1 hour   Servings: 4

Ingredients:

1 orange, zested and juiced
2 chipotle peppers, chopped
1 tablespoon balsamic vinegar
1 tablespoon molasses

1 teaspoon Dijon mustard
1 teaspoon salt
4 chicken breasts

Directions:

Mix the orange zest, orange juice, chipotle peppers, vinegar, molasses, mustard and salt in a bowl.

Brush the chicken with this mixture and place it in a deep dish baking pan.

Seal the pan with aluminum foil and cook in the preheated oven at 350F for 25 minutes then remove the foil and cook for 20 additional minutes.

Serve the chicken warm with your favorite side dish.

Nutritional information per serving

Calories: 313
Fat: 10.5g

Protein: 41.4g
Carbohydrates: 11.4g

$\mathcal{P}$ROSCIUTTO WRAPPED PRAWNS

Time: 20 minutes

Servings: 4

Ingredients:

16 fresh prawns

16 prosciutto slices

Directions:

Wrap each prawn with a slice of prosciutto.
Heat a grill pan over medium flame then place the prawns on the grill.
Cook on each side for 2 minutes.
Serve the prawns right away.

Nutritional information per serving

Calories: 196
Fat: 6.8g

Protein: 31.4g
Carbohydrates: 1.3g

$\mathcal{S}$ALMON ROSTI

Time: 25 minutes

Servings: 4

Ingredients:

2 salmon fillets
1 large potato, peeled and grated
1 carrot, peeled and grated
2 garlic cloves, minced
1 tablespoon chopped parsley

1 tablespoon chopped cilantro
1 teaspoon capers, chopped
Salt and pepper to taste
2 tablespoons virgin coconut oil

Directions:

Place the salmon fillets in a food processor and pulse until well mixed and ground.
Add the potato, carrot, garlic, parsley, cilantro and capers, as well as salt and pepper.
Mix well then form small patties.
Heat the oil in a skillet then place the rosti in the hot oil.
Fry on each side for 2-3 minutes until golden brown.
Remove the rosti on paper towels and serve right away.

Nutritional information per serving

Calories: 258
Fat: 12.6g

Protein: 19.4g
Carbohydrates: 18.2g

$\mathcal{A}$PRICOT ROASTED CHICKEN

Time: 1 hour   Servings: 4

Ingredients:

4 chicken breasts
Salt and pepper to taste
1 pound apricots, halved and pitted
½ cup chicken stock

¼ cup dry white wine
1 rosemary sprig
1 thyme sprig

Directions:

Season the chicken with salt and pepper and place it in a deep dish baking pan.
Add the apricots, stock, wine, rosemary sprig and thyme and adjust the taste with salt and pepper.
Cover the pan with aluminum foil and cook in the preheated oven at 350F for 30 minutes.
Remove the foil and cook for another 20 minutes.
Serve the chicken warm and fresh.

Nutritional information per serving

Calories: 334   Protein: 42.1g
Fat: 11.2g   Carbohydrates: 12.9g

$\mathcal{B}$LUE CHEESE SEARED STEAK

Time: 40 minutes   Servings: 2

Ingredients:

2 beef steaks
2 tablespoons extra virgin olive oil
Salt and pepper to taste

1 teaspoon dried thyme
1 teaspoon dried rosemary
2 oz. blue cheese, crumbled

Directions:

Brush beef with olive oil, then season with salt and pepper, as well as thyme and rosemary.
Heat a grill pan over medium flame and place the steaks on the grill.
Cook on each side for 5-6 minutes, depending on how well done you like it.
When done, remove from the grill and top with crumbled blue cheese while hot.
Serve right away.

Nutritional information per serving

Calories: 382   Protein: 32g
Fat: 27.6g   Carbohydrates: 1.4g

Grilled Salmon with Kale and Apple Salad

Time: 30 minutes

Servings: 4

Ingredients:

4 salmon fillets
Salt and pepper to taste
1 teaspoon smoked paprika
1 teaspoon cumin powder

6 kale leaves, shredded
2 green apples, peeled and sliced
2 tablespoons lemon juice

Directions:

Season the salmon with salt, pepper, paprika and cumin powder.
Heat a grill pan over medium flame then place the salmon on the grill. Cook on each side for 3-4 minutes.
In the meantime, make the salad by combining the kale, green apples and lemon juice in a salad bowl.
     Add salt and pepper to taste.
Serve the fish warm with kale salad.

Nutritional information per serving

Calories: 338
Fat: 11.4g

Protein: 38.0g
Carbohydrates: 23.8g

Lemon Spinach with Roasted Chicken

Time: 1 hour

Servings: 4

Ingredients:

4 chicken breasts
Salt and pepper to taste
1 teaspoon dried oregano
1 teaspoon dried basil

2 tablespoons extra virgin olive oil
2 garlic cloves, minced
1 pound baby spinach
1 lemon, juiced

Directions:

Season the chicken with salt, pepper, oregano and basil and place it in a deep dish baking pan.
Cover the pan with aluminum foil and cook in the preheated oven at 350F for 35 minutes.
While the chicken cooks, heat the oil in a saucepan.
Add the garlic and cook for 30 seconds then stir in the spinach and cook for 10 minutes on high heat.
Drizzle with lemon juice and serve the chicken with the lemon spinach.

Nutritional information per serving

Calories: 356
Fat: 17.9g

Protein: 43.5g
Carbohydrates: 4.9g

CHICKEN PARMESAN RISOTTO

Time: 45 minutes

Servings: 6

Ingredients:

2 tablespoons extra virgin olive oil
1 shallot, chopped
1 chicken breast, diced
¾ cup wild rice
2 tablespoons dry white wine

1½ cups chicken stock
1 cup green peas
Salt and pepper to taste
2 oz. grated Parmesan cheese

Directions:

Heat the oil in a skillet and stir in the shallot. Cook for 1 minute until softened then add the chicken and
    cook for 5 additional minutes.

Stir in the wild rice, wine, stock and green peas, as well as salt and pepper.

Cook on low heat for 20 minutes.

When done, stir in the cheese and serve the risotto warm.

Nutritional information per serving

Calories: 216
Fat: 8.2g

Protein: 16.7g
Carbohydrates: 19.4g

SPICY GLAZED SALMON WITH SAUTÉED CARROTS

Time: 30 minutes

Servings: 4

Ingredients

4 salmon fillets
Salt and pepper to taste
2 tablespoons hot sauce
2 tablespoons extra virgin olive oil

1 teaspoon cumin powder
¼ teaspoon ground coriander
1 pound carrots, sliced

Directions:

Season the salmon with salt and pepper and brush it with hot sauce.

Place the salmon in a baking tray lined with parchment paper.

Bake in the preheated oven at 350F for 10-15 minutes.

Heat the oil in a skillet and stir in the cumin and coriander, as well as carrots.

Add salt and pepper to taste and cook the carrots on medium flame until softened, about 10 minutes.

Serve the carrots warm with the spicy salmon.

Nutritional information per serving

Calories: 345
Fat: 18.1g

Protein: 35.6g
Carbohydrates: 11.5g

Butternut Squash Wholesome Pasta

Time: 35 minutes   Servings: 6

Ingredients:

2 tablespoons extra virgin olive oil
1 shallot, chopped
2 garlic cloves, minced
2 cups butternut squash cubes
1 cup diced tomatoes

¼ teaspoon red pepper flakes
½ cup vegetable stock
1 bay leaf
Salt and pepper to taste
12 oz. whole wheat spaghetti

Directions:

Heat the oil in a saucepan. Add the shallot and garlic and cook for 1 minute then stir in the rest of the
    ingredients except the spaghetti.
Season with salt and pepper and cook on low heat for 20 minutes.
In the meantime, pour a few cups of water in a pot and add a pinch of salt. Bring to a boil.
Throw in the pasta and cook for 8 minutes until al dente. Drain well.
Mix the pasta with the butternut squash sauce and serve the pasta warm.

Nutritional information per serving

Calories: 133   Protein: 3.7g
Fat: 5.2g   Carbohydrates: 20.4g

Spiced Eggplant Stew

Time: 45 minutes   Servings: 6

Ingredients:

2 tablespoons extra virgin olive oil
2 shallots, chopped
4 garlic cloves, minced
1 carrot, diced
1 parsnip, diced
1 turnip, peeled and diced
2 large eggplants, cubed

½ teaspoon cumin powder
¼ teaspoon chili powder
¼ teaspoon coriander powder
2 cups diced tomatoes
1 bay leaf
1 cup vegetable stock
Salt and pepper to taste

Directions:

Heat the oil in a saucepan and stir in the shallots, garlic, carrot, parsnip and turnip. Add the eggplants
    as well.
Cook for 5 minutes then add the spices, tomatoes, bay leaf and stock, as well as salt and pepper.
Cook on low heat for 30 minutes.
Serve the stew warm and fresh.

Nutritional information per serving

Calories: 92

Fat: 5.0g

Protein: 1.7g

Carbohydrates: 11.8g

Mediterranean Tomato Sauce

Time: 35 minutes

Servings: 4

Ingredients:

2 tablespoons extra virgin olive oil

2 garlic cloves, minced

2 shallots, chopped

1 pound tomatoes, peeled and sliced

1 cup vegetable stock

1 bay leaf

1 teaspoon dried basil

½ teaspoon dried oregano

Salt and pepper to taste

Directions:

Heat the oil in a saucepan and add the garlic and shallot. Cook for 2 minutes.

Stir in the rest of the ingredients and season with salt and pepper.

Cook on low heat for 20 minutes.

Serve the sauce fresh with whole wheat pasta.

Nutritional information per serving

Calories: 89

Fat: 7.3g

Protein: 1.4g

Carbohydrates: 6.3g

Tuna Orzo Salad

Time: 35 minutes

Servings: 4

Ingredients:

1 cup orzo

2 cups vegetable stock

2 tuna fillets

1 tablespoon soy sauce

2 tablespoons extra virgin olive oil

1 celery stalk, sliced

2 tablespoons chopped parsley

½ lemon, juiced

Salt and pepper to taste

Directions:

Combine the orzo with the stock in a saucepan and cook on low heat for 20-25 minutes until all the liquid has been absorbed.

Transfer the orzo in a salad bowl.

Brush the tuna with the soy sauce and oil.

Heat a grill pan over medium flame and place the tuna on the grill. Cook on each side for 2 minutes then cut into cubes.

Mix the orzo with the tuna, celery, parsley and lemon juice and adjust the taste with salt and pepper. Serve the salad fresh.

Nutritional information per serving

Calories: 407
Fat: 23.4g

Protein: 16.3g
Carbohydrates: 32.9g

TAGLIATELLE WITH CHICKEN AND RICOTTA CHEESE

Time: 35 minutes

Servings: 6

Ingredients:

2 tablespoons extra virgin olive oil
2 chicken breasts, diced
2 garlic cloves, minced
½ cup green peas

1 cup chicken stock
Salt and pepper to taste
12 oz. tagliatelle
1 cup ricotta cheese

Directions:

Heat the oil in a skillet and stir in the chicken. Cook for 10 minutes.
Add the garlic, green peas and stock and season with salt and pepper.
Cook for another 10 minutes.
In the meantime, pour a few cups of water in a pot and add a pinch of salt. Add the tagliatelle and cook for 8 minutes then drain well.
When the chicken is done and reduced, stir in the ricotta and remove from heat.
Stir in the tagliatelle and mix well.
Serve the pasta warm.

Nutritional information per serving

Calories: 408
Fat: 13.5g

Protein: 20.4g
Carbohydrates: 50g

CHICKEN MARSALA

Time: 40 minutes

Servings: 4

Ingredients:

4 chicken fillets
Salt and pepper to taste
1 tablespoon cornstarch
2 tablespoons extra virgin olive oil

2 prosciutto slices, chopped
1 pound button mushrooms
¼ cup Marsala wine
1 cup chicken stock

Directions:

Season the chicken with salt and pepper then sprinkle with cornstarch.

Heat the oil in a saucepan and place the chicken in the hot oil.
Cook on each side until golden then add the rest of the ingredients.
Season with salt and pepper and cook on low heat for 25 minutes.
Serve the chicken and the sauce warm.

Nutritional information per serving

Calories: 383

Fat: 17.8g

Protein: 44.2g

Carbohydrates: 6.1g

Grilled Tomato Soup with Parmesan Cheese

Time: 50 minutes

Servings: 8

Ingredients:

2 pounds tomatoes, halved
2 tablespoons extra virgin olive oil
1 teaspoon dried thyme
1 teaspoon dried oregano
1 teaspoon dried basil
2 sweet onions, chopped

2 garlic cloves, minced
2 cups vegetable stock
4 cups water
1 tablespoon balsamic vinegar
Salt and pepper to taste
Grated Parmesan for serving

Directions:

Place the tomatoes on a baking tray lined with parchment paper.
Drizzle with olive oil and sprinkle with dried herbs.
Bake in the preheated oven at 400F for 20 minutes or until slightly caramelized.
Transfer the tomatoes in a pot and add the rest of the ingredients.
Season with salt and pepper and cook on low heat for 15 minutes.
When done, remove from heat and puree the soup with an immersion blender.
Serve the soup warm, topped with grated cheese.

Nutritional information per serving

Calories: 85

Fat: 3.8g

Protein: 1.5g

Carbohydrates: 7.7g

Celeriac Quinoa Pilaf with Chicken Thighs

Time: 45 minutes

Servings: 6

Ingredients:

6 chicken thighs
Salt and pepper to taste
1 cup quinoa, rinsed
2 celery roots, peeled and diced
1 shallot, chopped

2 garlic cloves, minced
2 green bell peppers, cored and diced
1 yellow bell pepper, cored and diced
1 teaspoon dried basil
2 cups vegetable stock

Directions:

Season the chicken with salt and pepper.
Combine the quinoa, celery roots, shallot, garlic, bell peppers, basil and stock in a deep dish baking pan.
Season with salt and pepper then place the chicken on top.
Bake in the preheated oven at 350F for 35-40 minutes.
Serve the chicken and quinoa warm.

Nutritional information per serving

Calories: 414
Fat: 12.5g

Protein: 46.1g
Carbohydrates: 27.2g

Chicken in Lime Cilantro Sauce

Time: 50 minutes

Servings: 2

Ingredients:

2 chicken breasts
Salt and pepper to taste
2 tablespoons extra virgin olive oil

1 lime, sliced
1 cup chopped cilantro
1 cup chicken stock

Directions:

Season the chicken with salt and pepper.
Heat the oil in a skillet and add the chicken. Cook on all sides until golden.
Add the rest of the ingredients and cover the skillet with a lid.
Cook on low heat for 25 minutes.
Serve the chicken and sauce warm.

Nutritional information per serving

Calories: 393
Fat: 24.7g

Protein: 41g
Carbohydrates: 0.7g

Greek Chicken with Rice Salad

Time: 1 hour

Servings: 6

Ingredients:

6 chicken thighs
Salt and pepper to taste
1 teaspoon dried basil
1 teaspoon dried oregano
½ teaspoon celery powder
1 tablespoon lemon zest
½ cup wild rice

1½ cups vegetable stock
1 cup cherry tomatoes, halved
½ cup chopped parsley
2 garlic cloves, minced
1 red onion, sliced
1 cucumber, sliced
1 lemon, juiced

Directions:

Season the chicken thighs with salt, pepper, basil, oregano, celery powder and lemon zest.
Place the chicken in a deep dish baking pan and cook in the preheated oven at 350F for 40 minutes.
For the salad, cook the rice in stock until the liquid has been completely absorbed.
When done, transfer the rice in a salad bowl and add the rest of the ingredients.
Adjust the taste of the salad with salt and pepper and mix well.
Serve the chicken with salad.

Nutritional information per serving

Calories: 339
Fat: 10.7g

Protein: 43.5g
Carbohydrates: 15.7g

Sun-Dried Tomato Chicken

Time: 1 hour

Servings: 4

Ingredients:

4 oz. sun-dried tomatoes, chopped
2 jalapeños, chopped
4 garlic cloves, minced
4 oz. baby spinach, shredded

Salt and pepper to taste
4 chicken breasts
½ cup dry white wine

Directions:

Mix the sun-dried tomatoes, jalapeños, garlic, spinach, salt and pepper in a bowl.
Cut a small pocket into each chicken breast and stuff it with the tomato mixture.
Place the chicken in a deep dish baking pan and pour in the wine.
Cover the pan with aluminum foil and bake in the preheated oven at 350F for 20 minutes then remove the foil and cook for another 20 minutes.
Serve the chicken warm with your favorite side dish.

Nutritional information per serving

Calories: 310
Fat: 10.6g

Protein: 41.9g
Carbohydrates: 4.4g

Greek Tomato Chicken Stew

Time: 1 hour

Servings: 6

Ingredients:

2 tablespoons extra virgin olive oil
6 chicken thighs
4 garlic cloves, minced
1 sweet onion, chopped

2 red bell peppers, cored and sliced
1 yellow bell pepper, cored and sliced
4 oz. sun-dried tomatoes, chopped
2 cups cherry tomatoes, halved

1½ cups chicken stock
1 bay leaf

Salt and pepper to taste

Directions:

Heat the oil in a saucepan and add the chicken.

Cook on all sides until golden then add the garlic, onion and peppers and cook for 5 minutes until softened.

Stir in the rest of the ingredients and adjust the taste with salt and pepper.

Cook on low heat for 35 minutes.

Serve the chicken and sauce warm.

Nutritional information per serving

Calories: 351
Fat: 15.5g

Protein: 42.3g
Carbohydrates: 9.2g

COCONUT FLAKE CRUSTED CHICKEN

Time: 45 minutes

Servings: 6

Ingredients:

1 cup coconut milk
1 teaspoon chili powder
1 teaspoon lemon zest
¼ teaspoon cumin powder

1 teaspoon salt
6 chicken fillets
1 cup coconut flakes

Directions:

Mix the coconut milk, chili powder, lemon zest, cumin powder and salt in a bowl.

Dip the chicken into the coconut milk mixture then roll it through coconut flakes.

Place the chicken on a baking tray lined with parchment paper.

Bake in the preheated oven at 350F for 25 minutes.

Serve the chicken warm.

Nutritional information per serving

Calories: 407
Fat: 24.4g

Protein: 42g
Carbohydrates: 4.6g

CHICKEN BERRY SALAD

Time: 40 minutes

Servings: 6

Ingredients:

4 chicken fillets
Salt and pepper to taste

1 teaspoon dried oregano
1 teaspoon dried basil

Salt and pepper to taste
4 cups baby spinach
2 cups arugula
½ cup fresh strawberries

½ cup fresh raspberries
1 lemon, juiced
2 tablespoons extra virgin olive oil

Directions:

Season the chicken with salt, pepper, oregano and basil.

Heat a grill pan over medium flame and place the chicken on the grill.

Cook on each side for 4-5 minutes until golden brown and the juices run out clear.

When done, cut the chicken into thin strips.

Mix the spinach and arugula on a platter.

Top with chicken then make the dressing by combining the strawberries, raspberries, lemon juice, salt and pepper in a blender.

Add the olive oil and pulse until smooth and creamy.

Drizzle the dressing over the salad and serve right away.

Nutritional information per serving

Calories: 234
Fat: 11.9g

Protein: 28g
Carbohydrates: 3.3g

Chicken Thighs with Pepper Salsa

Time: 1 hour

Servings: 6

Ingredients:

2 tablespoons extra virgin olive oil
2 garlic cloves, minced
1 sweet onion, sliced
2 red bell peppers, cored and sliced
2 yellow bell peppers, cored and sliced
2 green bell peppers, cored and sliced
½ cup chopped parsley
¼ cup chopped cilantro

1 jalapeño pepper, chopped
1 cup tomato juice
1 cup chicken stock
1 teaspoon dried basil
1 thyme sprig
6 chicken thighs
Salt and pepper to taste

Directions:

Heat the oil in a skillet then stir in the garlic and onion. Cook for 1 minute until softened then stir in the peppers, parsley, cilantro, jalapeño, tomato juice, stock, basil and thyme.

Top with the chicken thighs and season with salt and pepper.

Cook in the preheated oven at 350F for 40 minutes.

Serve the chicken and the sauce warm.

Nutritional information per serving

Calories: 363
Fat: 15.2g

Protein: 42.0g
Carbohydrates: 11.5g

Mustard Tarragon Chicken Casserole

Time: 1 hour

Servings: 6

Ingredients:

6 chicken drumsticks
Salt and pepper to taste
2 tablespoons Dijon mustard
1 teaspoon dried tarragon
2 zucchinis, sliced
1 eggplant, peeled and cubed
2 red bell peppers, cored and sliced

1 shallot, sliced
4 garlic cloves, minced
1 lemon, juiced
¼ cup dry white wine
1 can diced tomatoes
1 cup chicken stock

Directions:

Season the chicken with salt and pepper, as well as the mustard and tarragon.

Combine the zucchinis, eggplant, bell peppers, shallot, garlic, lemon juice, wine, tomatoes and stock in a deep dish baking pan.

Add the chicken on top and adjust the taste with salt and pepper.

Cook in the preheated oven at 350F for 35-40 minutes.

Serve the casserole warm and fresh.

Nutritional information per serving

Calories: 243
Fat: 3.4g

Protein: 15.4g
Carbohydrates: 12.2g

Okra Chicken Curry

Time: 1 hour

Servings: 6

Ingredients:

6 chicken drumsticks
1 tablespoon Dijon mustard
2 tablespoons extra virgin olive oil
1 teaspoon turmeric powder
1 teaspoon garlic powder
1 teaspoon ground coriander
1 teaspoon cumin powder
1 teaspoon curry powder

1 bay leaf
1 thyme sprig
1 head cauliflower, cut into florets
1 pound okra, trimmed and halved
1 cup diced tomatoes
1½ cups chicken stock
Salt and pepper to taste

Directions:

Brush the chicken with Dijon mustard.

Heat the oil in a deep saucepan and add the chicken. Cook on all sides until fragrant and golden then stir in the spices and herbs and cook for 30 seconds just until fragrant.

Add the vegetables and stock and season with salt and pepper.
Cook on low heat for 30 minutes.
Serve the curry warm.

Nutritional information per serving

Calories: 194
Fat: 7.9g

Protein: 15.7g
Carbohydrates: 10.4g

CHICKEN TOMATILLO STEW

Time: 1 hour

Servings: 6

Ingredients:

2 tablespoons extra virgin olive oil
6 chicken thighs
1 sweet onion, chopped
2 garlic cloves, minced
1 jalapeño pepper, chopped
2 green chile, chopped
½ teaspoon cumin powder

¼ teaspoon chili powder
1 can tomatillos, drained and chopped
½ cup chopped cilantro
½ cup chopped parsley
1 cup chicken stock
Salt and pepper to taste

Directions:

Heat the oil in a deep saucepan and place the chicken. Cook on all sides until golden then stir in the onion, garlic, jalapeño, green chile and spices.
Cook for 2 minutes until softened then add the tomatillos, cilantro, parsley and stock, as well as salt and pepper.
Cook on low heat for 35 minutes.
Serve the stew warm and fresh.

Nutritional information per serving

Calories: 328
Fat: 15.4g

Protein: 41.5g
Carbohydrates: 4.6g

BUTTON MUSHROOM STEW

Time: 30 minutes

Servings: 4

Ingredients:

2 tablespoons extra virgin olive oil
1 chicken breast, cubed
2 prosciutto slices, chopped
1 shallot, chopped
2 garlic cloves, minced

1 pound button mushrooms
1 cup chicken stock
Salt and pepper to taste

Directions:

Heat the oil in a saucepan and add the chicken and prosciutto. Cook for 5 minutes on all sides.

Add the rest of the ingredients and season with salt and pepper.

Cook on low heat for 30 minutes, adding more liquid if necessary.

Serve the stew warm and fresh.

Nutritional information per serving

Calories: 253

Fat: 14.3g

Protein: 29.1g

Carbohydrates: 4.8g

CHICKEN CAPRESE

Time: 35 minutes

Servings: 4

Ingredients:

4 chicken breasts

Salt and pepper to taste

2 tablespoons extra virgin olive oil

1 pound cherry tomatoes

½ cup dry white wine

1 rosemary sprig

1 thyme sprig

4 slices mozzarella

Directions:

Season the chicken with salt and pepper.

Heat the oil in a skillet that can go in the oven.

Add the chicken and cook on all sides until golden brown.

Add the cherry tomatoes, wine, rosemary and thyme.

Cook in the preheated oven at 350F for 30 minutes.

When done, top each chicken breast with mozzarella and serve fresh and warm.

Nutritional information per serving

Calories: 451

Fat: 22.6g

Protein: 49.5g

Carbohydrates: 6.2g

BUTTERMILK MARINATED CHICKEN

Time: 1¾ hours

Servings: 4

Ingredients:

4 chicken breasts

Salt and pepper to taste

1 cup buttermilk

1 teaspoon lemon zest

1 teaspoon coriander seeds

1 teaspoon cumin seeds

½ teaspoon smoked paprika

½ teaspoon chili powder

1 tablespoon lemon juice

½ cup chicken stock

Directions:

Season the chicken with salt and pepper and place it in a zip lock bag.

Add the rest of the ingredients and seal the bag.

Place in the fridge to marinate the chicken for 1 hour at least.

Transfer the chicken in a deep dish baking pan and cover with aluminum foil.

Cook in the preheated oven at 350F for 30 minutes then remove the foil and cook for 10 additional minutes.

Serve the chicken warm with your favorite side dish.

Nutritional information per serving

Calories: 297

Fat: 11.2g

Protein: 42.8g

Carbohydrates: 3.8g

Cauliflower Quinoa Casserole

Time: 45 minutes

Servings: 6

Ingredients:

¾ cup quinoa, rinsed

1 head cauliflower, cut into florets

2 cups vegetable stock

1 celery stalk, sliced

2 tablespoons pesto sauce

2 cups baby spinach

2 green onions, sliced

Salt and pepper to taste

2 oz. grated Parmesan cheese

Directions:

Combine the quinoa, cauliflower, stock, celery, pesto sauce, spinach and green onions in a deep dish baking pan.

Add salt and pepper and mix well.

Cover the casserole with aluminum foil and bake in the preheated oven at 350F for 25 minutes.

Sprinkle on top with cheese and bake for 5 additional minutes without the foil to cover it.

Serve the casserole warm.

Nutritional information per serving

Calories: 149

Fat: 5.6g

Protein: 7.9g

Carbohydrates: 17.8g

Coconut Quinoa Lentil Curry

Time: 1 hour

Servings: 8

Ingredients:

2 tablespoons extra virgin olive oil

1 sweet onion, chopped

4 garlic cloves, minced

1 jalapeño pepper, chopped

1 celery stalk, sliced

1 carrot, diced

1 teaspoon curry powder
½ teaspoon cumin powder
¼ teaspoon chili powder
½ cup quinoa, rinsed
½ cup green quinoa
1 can diced tomatoes

1 ½ cups vegetable stock
1 cup coconut milk
1 bay leaf
2 kaffir lime leaves
Salt and pepper to taste
Chopped cilantro for serving

Directions:

Heat the oil in a deep saucepan and stir in the onion, garlic and jalapeño pepper. Cook for 1 minute until softened then stir in the rest of the ingredients.

Adjust the taste with salt and pepper and cook on low heat for 35-40 minutes.

Serve the curry warm and fresh, topped with chopped cilantro.

Nutritional information per serving

Calories: 157
Fat: 11.4g

Protein: 2.7g
Carbohydrates: 12.8g

BUTTERNUT SQUASH TOMATO GRATIN

Time: 1 hour

Servings: 6

Ingredients:

1 sweet onion, sliced
4 garlic cloves, minced
4 cups butternut squash cubes
2 tomatoes, sliced
½ teaspoon dried basil

Salt and pepper to taste
½ cup unsweetened shredded coconut
½ cup grated Parmesan cheese
2 tablespoons extra virgin olive oil

Directions:

Layer the onion, garlic, butternut squash cubes, tomatoes, basil, salt and pepper in a deep dish baking pan. Top with the coconut and cheese then drizzle with oil.

Bake in the preheated oven at 350F for 35-40 minutes.

Serve the gratin fresh and warm.

Nutritional information per serving

Calories: 159
Fat: 11.1g

Protein: 3.5g
Carbohydrates: 12.8g

BUTTERNUT SQUASH CURRY

Time: 1 hour

Servings: 6

Ingredients:

2 tablespoons extra virgin olive oil

1 sweet onion, chopped

2 garlic cloves, minced
1 celery stalk, chopped
1 jalapeño pepper, chopped
1 teaspoon curry powder
2 tablespoons tomato paste
1 cup diced tomatoes

4 cups butternut squash cubes
1 cup vegetable stock
1 bay leaf
Salt and pepper to taste
½ cup coconut milk for serving

Directions:

Heat the oil in a deep saucepan and stir in the onion, garlic, celery and pepper. Cook for 2 minutes until softened then stir in the curry powder, tomato paste and tomatoes.

Add the butternut squash cubes, stock and bay leaf, as well as salt and pepper.

Cook on low heat for 30 minutes.

Serve the curry drizzled with coconut milk.

Nutritional information per serving

Calories: 135
Fat: 9.6g

Protein: 2.0g
Carbohydrates: 12.6g

 RILLED TOMATO FARRO SALAD

Time: 35 minutes

Servings: 6

Ingredients:

2 garlic cloves, minced
2 tablespoons extra virgin olive oil
1 teaspoon dried basil
¾ cup farro, rinsed
1¾ cups vegetable stock
Salt and pepper to taste

2 tablespoons lemon juice
1 pound tomatoes, sliced

¼ cup chopped parsley
1 tablespoon balsamic vinegar

Directions:

Mix the garlic, oil, basil and lemon juice in a bowl. Brush the tomatoes with this mixture.

Heat a grill pan over medium flame then place the tomatoes on the grill.

Cook on each side for 1-2 minutes until browned.

Combine the farro and stock in a saucepan. Add salt and pepper and cook on low heat until the liquid is completely absorbed, about 20 minutes.

Transfer the farro in a salad bowl. Add the tomatoes, parsley and vinegar and mix well.

Serve the salad right away.

Nutritional information per serving

Calories: 143
Fat: 5.4g

Protein: 4.3g
Carbohydrates: 19.6g

Balsamic Grilled Vegetable Salad

Time: 35 minutes

Servings: 4

Ingredients:

1 zucchini, sliced
1 sweet potato, peeled and sliced
2 tomatoes, sliced
1 parsnip, peeled and sliced
1 carrot, sliced
2 tablespoons extra virgin olive oil

1 teaspoon dried oregano
1 teaspoon dried basil
Salt and pepper to taste
2 tablespoons balsamic vinegar
2 tablespoons chopped parsley

Directions:

Combine the zucchini, sweet potato, tomatoes, parsnip, carrots, olive oil, oregano and basil in a bowl.
    Add salt and pepper as well.
Heat a grill pan over medium flame and place the vegetables on the grill.
Cook on each side for 2-3 minutes until browned then transfer them in a salad bowl.
Add the vinegar and parsley and mix well.
Serve the salad fresh.

Nutritional information per serving

Calories: 139
Fat: 7.4g

Protein: 2.3g
Carbohydrates: 17.9g

Spiced Lentil Stew

Time: 45 minutes

Servings: 4

Ingredients:

2 tablespoons extra virgin olive oil
1 shallot, chopped
2 garlic cloves, minced
½ teaspoon cumin powder
½ teaspoon chili powder
½ teaspoon ground coriander
¼ teaspoon ground ginger
2 tablespoons tomato paste

1 celery stalk, sliced
2 carrots, diced
1 cup brown lentils
2 cups vegetable stock
1 bay leaf
1 red chili, sliced
Salt and pepper to taste

Directions:

Heat the oil in a heavy saucepan and stir in the shallot and garlic. Cook for 30 seconds then add the spices,
    tomato paste, celery, carrots, lentils, stock, bay leaf and red chili.
Adjust the taste with salt and pepper and cook on low heat for 30 minutes.
Serve the stew warm and fresh.

Nutritional information per serving

Calories: 117
Fat: 7.4g

Protein: 2.7g
Carbohydrates: 11.4g

GARLIC STUFFED CHICKEN

Time: 1 hour

Servings: 4

Ingredients:

4 chicken breasts
Salt and pepper to taste
12 garlic cloves, minced

2 thyme sprigs
1 rosemary sprig
1 cup dry white wine

Directions:

Season the chicken with salt and pepper then cut 3 small pockets into each chicken breast.
Stuff the chicken with garlic then place the chicken in a deep dish baking pan.
Add the thyme sprigs, rosemary and wine.
Bake in the preheated oven at 350F for 40 minutes.
Serve the chicken warm with your favorite side dish.

Nutritional information per serving

Calories: 328
Fat: 10.4g

Protein: 41.1g
Carbohydrates: 4.6g

BALSAMIC BRAISED CHICKEN

Time: 1 hour

Servings: 6

Ingredients:

6 chicken thighs
Salt and pepper to taste
1 teaspoon garlic powder
½ teaspoon onion powder

1 teaspoon dried thyme
1 teaspoon dried basil
¼ cup chicken stock
¼ cup balsamic vinegar

Directions:

Season chicken with salt and pepper, as well as garlic powder, onion powder, thyme and basil.
Place the chicken in a deep dish baking pan and pour in the stock and vinegar.
Cook in the preheated oven at 350F for 40 minutes.
Serve the chicken warm with your favorite side dish.

Nutritional information per serving

Calories: 271
Fat: 10.4g

Protein: 40.7g
Carbohydrates: 1g

ROSEMARY CHICKEN KABOBS

Time: 1 hour

Servings: 4

Ingredients:

1½ pounds chicken breasts, cubed
Salt and pepper to taste
1 tablespoon dried rosemary

1 teaspoon smoked paprika
1 zucchini, cubed
1 red onion, cut into large cubes

Directions:

Season the chicken with salt, pepper, rosemary and paprika.
Place the chicken, zucchini and red onion on wooden skewers.
Heat a grill pan over medium flame and place the kabobs on the grill.
Cook on each side for 4-5 minutes or more, until the juices of the chicken run out clean.
Serve the kabobs warm.

Nutritional information per serving

Calories: 346
Fat: 12.9g

Protein: 50.2g
Carbohydrates: 5.1g

LENTIL MEATBALL STEW

Time: 1 hour

Servings: 8

Ingredients:

1 pound ground beef
4 garlic cloves, minced
2 shallots, chopped
1 jalapeño, chopped
¼ teaspoon cumin powder
2 tablespoons chopped parsley

Salt and pepper to taste
2 tablespoons extra virgin olive oil
2 tomatoes, peeled and diced
½ cup brown lentils
1½ cups chicken stock

Directions:

For the meatballs, mix the ground beef, garlic, half of the chopped shallot, jalapeño, cumin powder, parsley, salt and pepper in a bowl. Mix well then form small meatballs.
Heat the oil in a skillet and stir in the rest of the shallot, tomatoes, lentils and stock. Season with salt and pepper.
Place the meatballs over the lentils and cook on low heat for 35 minutes.
Serve the lentils and meatballs warm and fresh.

Nutritional information per serving

Calories: 155
Fat: 7.3g

Protein: 18.2g
Carbohydrates: 3.7g

Chicken Tikka Masala

Time: 1 hour

Servings: 8

Ingredients:

2 tablespoons extra virgin olive oil
8 chicken thighs
1 teaspoon grated ginger
½ teaspoon cumin powder
½ teaspoon chili powder
¼ teaspoon cumin powder
4 garlic cloves, minced
1 jalapeño pepper, chopped

1 can diced tomatoes
1 cup coconut milk
1 cup chicken stock
1 thyme sprig
1 bay leaf
Salt and pepper to taste
Chopped cilantro for serving

Directions:

Heat the oil in a deep saucepan and add the chicken. Cook on each side until golden brown then stir in the rest of the ingredients.

Adjust the taste with salt and pepper.

Cook on low heat for 35-40 minutes until thickened and fragrant.

Serve the dish warm, topped with chopped cilantro.

Nutritional information per serving

Calories: 381
Fat: 21.2g

Protein: 41.5g
Carbohydrates: 2.7g

Apple Roasted Beef

Time: 1½ hours

Servings: 6

Ingredients:

2 pounds beef roast
Salt and pepper to taste
2 red apples, peeled and sliced
1 cup applesauce

1 cup apple juice
1 bay leaf
1 thyme sprig

Directions:

Season the beef roast with salt and pepper and place it in a deep dish baking pan.

Add the apples, applesauce, apple juice, bay leaf and thyme.

Cover the pan with aluminum foil and cook in the preheated oven at 350F for 1 hour.

Remove the foil and cook for another 20 minutes.

Serve the beef warm and fresh.

Nutritional information per serving

Calories: 359
Fat: 9.6g

Protein: 46.1g
Carbohydrates: 17.8g

Chicken in Tomato Lime Sauce

Time: 1 hour

Servings: 4

Ingredients:

2 tablespoons extra virgin olive oil
1 shallot, chopped
2 garlic cloves, minced
2 tablespoons tomato paste
1 celery stalk, chopped

4 chicken breasts
1½ cups chicken stock
Salt and pepper to taste
1 lime, sliced

Directions:

Heat the oil in a deep saucepan.
Add the shallot, garlic, tomato paste and celery and cook for 2 minutes.
Stir in the chicken, stock, salt and pepper and place over low heat.
Top the chicken with lime slices and cook on low heat for 35-40 minutes.
Serve the chicken and sauce warm and fresh.

Nutritional information per serving

Calories: 346
Fat: 17.7g

Protein: 41.4g
Carbohydrates: 4.6g

Spicy Beef Bell Peppers

Time: 1½ hours

Servings: 6

Ingredients:

6 red bell peppers
2 cups ground beef
2 tablespoons chopped dill
1 tablespoon chopped parsley
2 garlic cloves, minced
½ teaspoon smoked paprika
½ teaspoon chili powder

2 tablespoons tomato paste
½ cup wild rice
1 egg yolk
Salt and pepper to taste
1 cup diced tomatoes
1½ cups beef stock

Directions:

Cut off the top of each bell pepper and carefully remove the core.
Mix the beef, dill, parsley, garlic, paprika and chili, as well as tomato paste, rice and egg yolk in a bowl.
Add salt and pepper to taste and mix well.
Stuff each bell pepper with the beef mixture then place the peppers in a deep dish baking pan.
Pour in the tomatoes and stock and cover the pan with aluminum foil.
Bake in the preheated oven at 350F for 1 hour.
Serve the dish warm and fresh.

Nutritional information per serving

Calories: 271

Fat: 6.9g

Protein: 29.4g

Carbohydrates: 20.6g

LEMON PEPPER BRAISED CHICKEN

Time: 1 hour

Servings: 4

Ingredients:

4 chicken breasts

Salt and pepper to taste

1 lemon, sliced

2 jalapeño peppers, chopped

4 garlic cloves, minced

1 cup chicken stock

2 kaffir lime leaves

Directions:

Season the chicken with salt and pepper and place it in a deep dish baking pan.

Add the rest of the ingredients and cover the pan with aluminum foil.

Cook in the preheated oven at 350F for 30 minutes then remove the foil and cook for 15 additional minutes.

Serve the chicken warm with your favorite side dish.

Nutritional information per serving

Calories: 276

Fat: 10.6g

Protein: 41g

Carbohydrates: 1.7g

SESAME CRUSTED TUNA STEAKS

Time: 25 minutes

Servings: 2

Ingredients:

2 tuna steaks

Salt and pepper to taste

2 tablespoons extra virgin olive oil

1 teaspoon sesame oil

2 tablespoons sesame seeds

Directions:

Season the steaks with salt and pepper.

Drizzle the tuna with oil and rub it well.

Sprinkle with sesame seeds.

Heat a grill pan over medium flame then place the tuna on the grill.

Cook on each side for 2-3 minutes.

Serve the tuna steaks warm with your favorite side dish.

Nutritional information per serving

Calories: 348

Fat: 26.1g

Protein: 27.1g

Carbohydrates: 2.1g

TOMATO BLACK OLIVE SHRIMPS

Time: 45 minutes

Servings: 6

Ingredients:

2 tablespoons extra virgin olive oil
2 garlic cloves, minced
1 shallot, chopped
2 red bell peppers, cored and sliced
1 can diced tomatoes
¼ cup dry white wine

1 pound fresh shrimps, peeled and deveined
1 cup black olives, pitted
½ teaspoon dried oregano
½ teaspoon dried basil
Salt and pepper to taste

Directions:

Heat the oil in a skillet and stir in the garlic, shallot and bell peppers.
Cook for 2 minutes until softened then stir in the tomatoes, wine, shrimps, black olives and herbs, as well as salt and pepper to taste.
Cook on low heat for 20 minutes.
Serve the dish warm and fresh.

Nutritional information per serving

Calories: 182
Fat: 8.5g

Protein: 18.1g
Carbohydrates: 6.5g

SPICY SALMON WITH BOK CHOY SAUTÉ

Time: 45 minutes

Servings: 4

Ingredients:

4 salmon fillets
Salt and pepper to taste
1 teaspoon smoked paprika
¼ teaspoon chili powder

2 bok choy, shredded
2 tablespoons extra virgin olive oil
1 tablespoon soy sauce

Directions:

Season the salmon with salt, pepper, paprika and chili powder.
Heat a grill pan over medium flame and place the salmon on the grill.
Cook on each side for 4-5 minutes.
Heat the oil in a skillet and stir in the bok choy. Cook for 5 minutes until softened then add the soy sauce and remove from heat.
Serve the bok choy and salmon right away.

Nutritional information per serving

Calories: 304
Fat: 18.2g

Protein: 35.4g
Carbohydrates: 1.5g

CREAMY CUCUMBER AND SALMON SALAD

Time: 40 minutes

Servings: 4

Ingredients:

4 salmon fillets
Salt and pepper to taste
¼ teaspoon cayenne pepper
1 lemon, sliced

2 cucumbers, sliced
½ cup low fat plain yogurt
1 teaspoon apple cider vinegar
1 tablespoon chopped dill

Directions:

Season the salmon with salt, pepper and cayenne pepper.

Pour a few cups of water in a saucepan and bring to a boil, adding the lemon slices as well. Add the salmon and cook for 4 minutes then drain well.

Cut the fish fillets into cubes and place them in a salad bowl.

Add the cucumber, yogurt, vinegar and dill and mix well, adjusting the taste with salt and pepper.

Nutritional information per serving

Calories: 282
Fat: 11.6g

Protein: 37.3g
Carbohydrates: 9.6g

GRILLED ZUCCHINI AND CHICKEN SALAD

Time: 35 minutes

Servings: 4

Ingredients:

2 chicken fillets
2 zucchinis, sliced
Salt and pepper to taste
1 teaspoon dried thyme
1 teaspoon dried oregano

1 teaspoon dried basil
2 tablespoons extra virgin olive oil
1 garlic clove, minced
1 lemon, juiced

Directions:

Season the chicken and zucchini with salt, pepper, thyme, oregano and basil.

Drizzle with olive oil then heat a grill pan over medium flame.

Add the chicken and zucchinis on the grill and cook on each side until golden brown.

Transfer the chicken and zucchinis in a salad bowl and add the garlic and lemon juice.

Serve the salad right away.

Nutritional information per serving

Calories: 212
Fat: 12.4g

Protein: 21.6g
Carbohydrates: 4g

BULGUR BEAN SALAD

Time: 35 minutes

Servings: 4

Ingredients:

½ cup bulgur
1½ cups chicken stock
Salt and pepper to taste
1 can black beans, drained
1 can red beans, drained

½ cup chopped parsley
1 garlic clove, minced
1 lemon, juiced
1 teaspoon balsamic vinegar

Directions:

Combine the bulgur with stock in a saucepan and cook for 20-25 minutes until all the liquid has been absorbed.

Transfer the bulgur in a salad bowl then stir in the beans, parsley, garlic, lemon juice and vinegar.

Add salt and pepper and mix well.

Serve the salad fresh.

Nutritional information per serving

Calories: 392
Fat: 1.7g

Protein: 23.7g
Carbohydrates: 74.1g

GRILLED EGGPLANT BLACK BEAN SALAD

Time: 35 minutes

Servings: 4

Ingredients:

2 eggplants, peeled and sliced
Salt and pepper to taste
1 teaspoon dried oregano
1 teaspoon dried basil

2 tablespoons extra virgin olive oil
1 can black beans
2 tablespoons balsamic vinegar
¼ cup chopped cilantro

Directions:

Season the eggplants with salt, pepper, oregano and basil and drizzle with olive oil.

Heat a grill pan over medium flame and place the eggplant on the grill.

Cook on each side for a few minutes until browned then transfer the eggplant in a salad bowl.

Add the beans, vinegar and cilantro and mix well.

Serve the salad fresh and warm.

Nutritional information per serving

Calories: 297
Fat: 8.2g

Protein: 13.2g
Carbohydrates: 46.7g

FISHERMEN'S SOUP

Time: 50 minutes   Servings: 6

Ingredients:

2 tablespoons extra virgin olive oil
2 leeks, sliced
2 garlic cloves, minced
1 fennel bulb, sliced
1 can diced tomatoes
2 tablespoons sherry vinegar
2 cups vegetable stock

1 cup water
1 thyme sprig
1 bay leaf
Salt and pepper to taste
½ pound mussels, cleaned
1 pound cod fillets, cubed
½ cup black olives, pitted

Directions:

Heat the oil in a saucepan and add the leeks, garlic and fennel bulb. Cook for a few minutes until softened.
Add the tomatoes, vinegar, stock, water, thyme, bay leaf, salt and pepper and bring to a boil.
Cook for 15 minutes on low heat.
Add the mussels and cod, as well as olives and cook for another 10 minutes.
Serve the soup warm and fresh.

Nutritional information per serving

Calories: 172   Protein: 17.3g
Fat: 7.1g   Carbohydrates: 11.0g

ROASTED COD WITH SWEET POTATO PUREE

Time: 1 hour   Servings: 4

Ingredients:

4 cod fillets
Salt and pepper to taste
1 teaspoon dried oregano
1½ pounds sweet potatoes, peeled and cubed

½ teaspoon cumin powder
¼ teaspoon chili powder
2 tablespoons extra virgin olive oil

Directions:

Season the cod fillets with salt, pepper and dried oregano.
Place the cod fillets in a baking tray and bake in the preheated oven at 350F for 15 minutes.
For the sweet potato puree, place the potatoes in a saucepan.
Add water to cover the potatoes and cook on low heat for 20 minutes.
Drain well then place the potatoes in a bowl and mash them well. Add the cumin powder, chili and olive oil and mix well.
Serve the cod with the sweet potato puree.

Nutritional information per serving

Calories: 433
Fat: 10.4g

Protein: 62.7g
Carbohydrates: 47g

Poached Halibut with Sautéed Green Beans

Time: 45 minutes

Servings: 4

Ingredients:

1 lemon, sliced
1 chili pepper, sliced
Salt and pepper to taste
4 halibut fillets
1 pound green beans

2 tablespoons extra virgin olive oil
2 garlic cloves, minced
1 teaspoon lemon zest
1 tablespoon lemon juice

Directions:

Pour a few cups of water in a saucepan and add the lemon slices and chili pepper. Add salt and pepper and bring to a boil.

Add the halibut and cook for 5 minutes then drain the halibut well.

In the same water you poached the halibut, throw in the beans and cook for 5 additional minutes. Drain well.

Heat the oil in a skillet and add the beans, garlic, lemon zest and lemon juice. Add salt and pepper and cook for 2 additional minutes.

Serve the halibut and green beans warm.

Nutritional information per serving

Calories: 421
Fat: 13.9g

Protein: 62.9g
Carbohydrates: 10.2g

Caribbean Chicken Breasts

Time: 45 minutes

Servings: 2

Ingredients:

2 chicken breasts
Salt and pepper to taste
1 mango, peeled and diced
2 jalapeño pepper, chopped
1 lime, juiced

¼ teaspoon ground coriander
1 star anise
½ cup chicken stock
Salt and pepper to taste

Directions:

Combine the chicken and the remaining ingredients in a deep dish baking pan.

Add salt and pepper to taste and cover the pan with aluminum foil.

Cook in the preheated oven at 350F for 20 minutes. Remove the foil and cook for another 20 minutes. Serve the chicken breasts warm with the sauce and your favorite side dish.

Nutritional information per serving

Calories: 345
Fat: 10.9g

Protein: 41.4g
Carbohydrates: 18.7g

KALE PESTO RISOTTO

Time: 40 minutes

Servings: 6

Ingredients:

2 tablespoons extra virgin olive oil
1 shallot, chopped
1 garlic clove, minced
4 kale leaves, chopped
1 cup wild rice

2 tablespoons pesto sauce
¼ cup dry white wine
2 cups chicken stock
Salt and pepper to taste

Directions:

Heat the oil in a saucepan and stir in the shallot and garlic, as well as the kale. Cook for 2 minutes until softened.

Stir in the rice and cook for 2 additional minutes then add the pesto sauce, wine and stock, then season with salt and pepper.

Cook on low heat for 25-30 minutes until thickened and creamy.

Serve the risotto warm and fresh.

Nutritional information per serving

Calories: 193
Fat: 7.3g

Protein: 6.1g
Carbohydrates: 25.9g

SHALLOT BRAISED BEEF STEAKS

Time: 1 hour

Servings: 4

Ingredients:

4 beef steaks
Salt and pepper to taste
4 shallots, sliced
2 garlic cloves, chopped
1 carrot, sliced

1 rosemary sprig
1 thyme sprig
½ cup dry white wine
1 cup beef stock

Directions:

Season the beef steaks with salt and pepper.
Combine the shallots, garlic, carrot, rosemary, thyme, wine and beef stock in a deep dish baking pan.

Top the shallots with the beef steaks then cover with aluminum foil.

Cook in the preheated oven at 350F for 20 minutes then remove the foil and cook for 5 additional minutes.

Serve the steaks and sauce warm and fresh.

Nutritional information per serving

Calories: 195

Fat: 5.4g

Protein: 26.7g

Carbohydrates: 2.8g

Spicy Jasmine Rice Pilaf

Time: 45 minutes

Servings: 6

Ingredients:

2 tablespoons extra virgin olive oil

1 leek, sliced

1 small fennel bulb, chopped

1 garlic clove, minced

¼ teaspoon ground coriander

¼ teaspoon chili powder

¼ teaspoon cumin powder

1 cup jasmine rice

2 cups chicken stock

Salt and pepper to taste

Directions:

Heat the oil in a saucepan and stir in the leek, fennel and garlic. Cook for 2 minutes until softened.

Add the rest of the ingredients and season with salt and pepper.

Cook on low heat until the liquid is completely absorbed.

Serve the pilaf warm and fresh.

Nutritional information per serving

Calories: 165

Fat: 5.0g

Protein: 2.7g

Carbohydrates: 27.7g

Honey Glazed Carrots and Parsnips

Time: 40 minutes

Servings: 4

Ingredients:

1 pound carrots, sliced

½ pound parsnips, sliced

2 tablespoons extra virgin olive oil

2 tablespoons raw honey

1 orange, juiced

Salt and pepper to taste

Directions:

Combine all the ingredients in a bowl and add salt and pepper to taste. Toss around until evenly coated in honey, oil and orange juice.

Transfer the mixture in a baking tray lined with parchment paper.

Bake in the preheated oven at 350F for 25-30 minutes.

Serve the carrots and parsnips warm.

Calories: 203   Protein: 2.1g
Fat: 7.2g   Carbohydrates: 35.4g

ROASTED CHILI SHRIMPS

Time: 25 minutes   Servings: 4

Ingredients:

1½ pounds shrimps, peeled and deveined   4 garlic cloves, minced
2 chili peppers, chopped   2 tablespoons extra virgin olive oil
1 lime, juiced   Salt and pepper to taste

Directions:

Combine the shrimps, chili pepper, lime juice, garlic and oil in a baking pan.
Add salt and pepper to taste and cook in the preheated oven at 350F for 15 minutes.
Serve the shrimps warm.

Nutritional information per serving

Calories: 273   Protein: 39.1g
Fat: 9.9g   Carbohydrates: 5.5g

HALIBUT WITH ROSE WATER VINAIGRETTE

Time: 30 minutes   Servings: 4

Ingredients:

4 halibut fillets   2 garlic cloves, minced
Salt and pepper to taste   1 small orange, juiced
1 teaspoon dried thyme   1 tablespoon balsamic vinegar
2 tablespoons extra virgin olive oil   1 teaspoon rose water

Directions:

Season the halibut fillets with salt, pepper and thyme.
Heat the oil in a skillet and add the halibut in the hot oil.
Fry on each side for 2-3 minutes until golden.
Remove from heat and add the rest of the ingredients.
Serve the halibut and sauce warm.

Nutritional information per serving

Calories: 393   Protein: 60.9g
Fat: 13.8g   Carbohydrates: 3.5g

Skillet Chicken with Harissa Chickpeas

Time: 1 hour

Servings: 4

Ingredients:

2 tablespoons extra virgin olive oil
2 garlic cloves, minced
2 shallots, chopped
2 tablespoons harissa paste
2 tablespoons tomato paste
1 can chickpeas, drained

1 cup chicken stock
1 cup water
1 rosemary sprig
4 chicken breasts
Salt and pepper to taste
1 lemon, sliced

Directions:

Heat the oil in a skillet and add the garlic, shallots, harissa paste and tomato paste. Cook for 2 minutes until softened.

Add the chickpeas, stock, water, rosemary and chicken then adjust the taste with salt and pepper.

Top with lemon slices and cook in the preheated oven at 350F for 35-40 minutes.

Serve the dish warm.

Nutritional information per serving

Calories: 419
Fat: 20.6g

Protein: 50g
Carbohydrates: 32.5g

Broccoli White Bean Salad

Time: 30 minutes

Servings: 6

Ingredients:

2 cups water
Salt and pepper to taste
1 pound broccoli florets
1 can white beans, drained

½ cup chopped parsley
2 garlic cloves, minced
1 lemon, juiced
½ cup grated Parmesan cheese

Directions:

Pour the water in a saucepan and add salt and pepper to taste. Bring to a boil then throw in the broccoli.

Cook for 5 minutes then drain well and place in a salad bowl.

Stir in the beans, parsley, garlic, lemon juice and Parmesan and season with salt and pepper.

Mix well and serve the salad fresh.

Nutritional information per serving

Calories: 161
Fat: 1g

Protein: 10.2g
Carbohydrates: 26g

Thai Beef Stir-Fry

Time: 25 minutes

Servings: 4

Ingredients:

2 tablespoons peanut oil
1 pound skirt steaks, cut into thin strips
4 garlic cloves, chopped
1 red chili, sliced
1 teaspoon dried basil
2 carrots, cut into sticks

1 leek, sliced
1 lime, juiced
2 tablespoons soy sauce
1 teaspoon fish sauce
1 teaspoon raw honey
1 green onion, chopped

Directions:

Heat the peanut oil in a wok and stir in the beef. Cook for 5 minutes on high heat, stirring often.
Add the garlic, red chili, basil, carrots and leeks and cook for 5-8 additional minutes.
Stir in the lime juice, soy sauce, fish sauce, honey and green onion and mix well.
Serve the stir-fry warm.

Nutritional information per serving

Calories: 340
Fat: 18.3g

Protein: 31.8g
Carbohydrates: 11.5g

Chili Ground Beef Stir-Fry

Time: 25 minutes

Servings: 4

Ingredients:

2 tablespoons peanut oil
1 pound ground beef
1 shallot, chopped
4 garlic cloves, minced
1 red chili, chopped

2 red bell peppers, cored and sliced
1 yellow bell pepper, cored and sliced
2 tablespoons soy sauce
1 teaspoon rice vinegar

Directions:

Heat the oil in a skillet or frying pan then stir in the ground beef. Cook for 5 minutes on high flame, stirring often.
Add the shallot, garlic, red chili and bell peppers and cook for another 5 minutes.
Add the soy sauce and vinegar and serve the stir-fry warm.

Nutritional information per serving

Calories: 310
Fat: 14.1g

Protein: 36.1g
Carbohydrates: 7.6g

Turkey Spinach Patties

Time: 30 minutes

Servings: 6

Ingredients:

1 pound ground turkey
1 cup baby spinach, chopped
4 garlic cloves, minced
½ teaspoon dried basil

1 shallot, chopped
1 egg yolk
Salt and pepper to taste

Directions:

Mix the turkey with the spinach, garlic, basil, shallot and egg yolk in a bowl.
Add salt and pepper to taste and mix well.
Form 6 patties and place them aside.
Heat a grill pan over medium flame and place the patties on the grill.
Cook on each side for 4-5 minutes until browned.
Serve the turkey patties warm.

Nutritional information per serving

Calories: 162
Fat: 9.1g

Protein: 21.4g
Carbohydrates: 1.2g

Garlicky Salmon Kebabs

Time: 35 minutes

Servings: 4

Ingredients:

6 garlic cloves, minced
2 tablespoons chopped parsley
2 tablespoons extra virgin olive oil

Salt and pepper to taste
4 salmon fillets, cubed
1 lemon, sliced

Directions:

Mix the garlic, parsley, oil, salt and pepper in a bowl.
Brush this mixture over the salmon then layer the fish and lemon slices on wooden skewers.
Heat a grill pan over medium flame then place the kebabs on the grill.
Cook on all sides until browned.
Serve the kebabs warm and fresh.

Nutritional information per serving

Calories: 307
Fat: 18.1g

Protein: 35.0g
Carbohydrates: 3.0g

GRILLED CHICKEN WITH TOMATO VINAIGRETTE

Time: 30 minutes   Servings: 4

Ingredients:

4 chicken fillets
Salt and pepper to taste
1 teaspoon smoked paprika
2 tablespoons extra virgin olive oil
2 garlic cloves, minced

2 cups cherry tomatoes, halved
1 thyme sprig
1 rosemary sprig
¼ cup dry red wine
1 tablespoon red wine vinegar

Directions:

Season the chicken with salt, pepper and paprika.

Heat a grill pan over medium flame and place the chicken on the grill. Cook on each side for 8-10 minutes.

In the meantime, heat the oil in a skillet and add the garlic, tomatoes, thyme, rosemary, wine, vinegar and salt and pepper to taste. Bring to a boil and cook for 5 minutes.

Add the chicken and cook for another 5 minutes.

Serve the chicken and the sauce warm.

Nutritional information per serving

Calories: 359
Fat: 17.6g

Protein: 41.5g
Carbohydrates: 4.8g

SPICY LOBSTER SPAGHETTI

Time: 45 minutes   Servings: 6

Ingredients:

12 oz. whole wheat spaghetti
2 tablespoons extra virgin olive oil
1 shallot, chopped
½ red chili, sliced

2 garlic cloves, minced
1 pound cherry tomatoes, halved
½ pound lobster meat
Salt and pepper to taste

Directions:

Pour a few cups of water in a pot and add a pinch of salt. Add the spaghetti and cook for 8 minutes until al dente. Drain well.

Heat the oil in a skillet and add the rest of the ingredients.

Season with salt and pepper and cook for 10 minutes on low to medium heat.

When done, stir in the spaghetti and serve right away.

Nutritional information per serving

Calories: 160
Fat: 5.4g

Protein: 11.0g
Carbohydrates: 18.6g

Dessert Recipes

DARK CHOCOLATE COATED STRAWBERRIES

Time: 25 minutes   Servings: 4

Ingredients:

1 pound strawberries, washed and dried   ½ cup coconut flakes
8 oz. dark chocolate, melted

Directions:

Dip each strawberry into melted dark chocolate then roll through coconut flakes.
Place on a baking tray lined with parchment paper and allow to set.
Serve the strawberries fresh.

Nutritional information per serving

Calories: 375   Protein: 5.4g
Fat: 20.5g   Carbohydrates: 43.9g

CHOCOLATE OATMEAL PARFAITS

Time: 25 minutes   Servings: 4

Ingredients:

1 cup rolled oats   3 tablespoons raw honey
2 tablespoons sliced almonds   2 tablespoons cocoa powder
2 tablespoons raisins   2 tablespoons cornstarch
2 tablespoons dried cranberries   1 pinch salt
2 cups low fat milk   1 egg

Directions:

Mix the oats, almonds, raisins and cranberries in a bowl and place aside.
Combine the milk and honey in a saucepan and bring to a boil.
In a bowl, mix the cocoa powder, cornstarch, salt and egg then gradually pour in the hot milk and mix well.
Pour the mixture back into the saucepan and cook on low heat until thickened.
Allow the pudding to cool down.
Layer the pudding and the oatmeal mixture in serving glasses.
Serve right away.

Nutritional information per serving

Calories: 246   Protein: 9.5g
Fat: 5.5g   Carbohydrates: 42.7g

LMOND MACAROONS

Time: 35 minutes   Servings: 20

Ingredients:

½ cup sweetened condensed milk   1 pinch salt
14 oz. sweetened shredded coconut   2 egg whites
½ cup sliced almonds

Directions:

Mix the condensed milk, shredded coconut, almonds and salt in a bowl.
Whip the egg whites until stiff and fold the meringue into the coconut mixture.
Spoon the mixture on a baking tray lined with baking paper.
Bake in the preheated oven at 350F for 18-20 minutes until crisp and golden brown.
Serve the macaroons chilled.

Nutritional information per serving

Calories: 133   Protein: 2.1g
Fat: 7.8g   Carbohydrates: 15.3g

BLACKBERRY COBBLER

Time: 1 hour   Servings: 8

Ingredients:

1½ pounds fresh blackberries   1 cup whole wheat flour
1 tablespoon lemon juice   1 cup rolled oats
¼ cup maple syrup   2 tablespoons raw honey
1 tablespoon cornstarch   ¼ cup coconut oil, melted
¼ teaspoon ground ginger

Directions:

Combine the blackberries, lemon juice, maple syrup, cornstarch and ginger in a deep dish baking pan.
For the topping, combine the wheat flour, oats, honey and coconut oil in a bowl and mix well.
Spread this mixture over the blackberries and bake in the preheated oven at 350F for 35-40 minutes until
    the topping is golden brown and crisp.
Serve the cobbler chilled.

Nutritional information per serving

Calories: 237   Protein: 4.2g
Fat: 8.1g   Carbohydrates: 38.9g

PEACH BLACKBERRY YOGURT CUPS

Time: 40 minutes

Servings: 4

Ingredients:

1½ cups low fat yogurt
2 peaches, pitted and sliced
1 cup fresh blackberries

3 tablespoons raw honey
½ cup rolled oats

Directions:

Layer the yogurt, peaches, blackberries, honey and oats in serving bowls or glasses.
Serve the cups right away.

Nutritional information per serving

Calories: 187
Fat: 2.1g

Protein: 7.6g
Carbohydrates: 34.5g

PUMPKIN PIE PUDDING

Time: 30 minutes

Servings: 4

Ingredients:

2 cups low fat milk
½ cup pumpkin puree
¼ teaspoon cinnamon powder
¼ teaspoon ground star anise

1 egg
1 pinch salt
2 tablespoons cornstarch

Directions:

Combine all the ingredients in a saucepan.
Place on low heat and cook until thickened.
Remove from heat and pour in serving glasses.
Serve chilled.

Nutritional information per serving

Calories: 94
Fat: 2.4g

Protein: 5.9g
Carbohydrates: 12.5g

BLUEBERRY RED WINE GRANITA

Time: 4 hours

Servings: 8

Ingredients:

2 cups blueberries
2 cups red wine
1 teaspoon lemon juice

3 tablespoons raw honey
1 teaspoon orange zest
¼ cup fresh orange juice

Directions:

Combine all the ingredients in a blender and pulse until smooth.

Pour the mixture in a container and freeze for 3-4 hours.

To ensure a creamy texture, remove the container from the freezer from time to time and mix into it with a fork.

Serve the granita chilled.

Nutritional information per serving

Calories: 98

Fat: 0.2g

Protein: 0.4g

Carbohydrates: 14.2g

DRIED FRUIT BREAD PUDDING

Time: 1 hour

Servings: 6

Ingredients:

6 whole wheat bread slices, cubed
¼ cup raisins
¼ cup dried apricots, chopped
¼ cup dried cranberries
2 tablespoons raw honey

1½ cups low fat milk
3 eggs
1 teaspoon vanilla extract
1 teaspoon orange zest
1 teaspoon lemon zest

Directions:

Combine the bread slices and fruits in a deep dish baking pan.

Put the honey, milk, eggs, vanilla, orange zest and lemon zest in a bowl and mix well.

Pour this mixture over the bread and allow to soak up for a few minutes.

Bake in the preheated oven at 350F for 30-40 minutes until set and golden brown.

Serve the pudding chilled.

Nutritional information per serving

Calories: 174

Fat: 3.8g

Protein: 8.8g

Carbohydrates: 26.7g

STRAWBERRY RHUBARB CRUSTLESS PIE

Time: 1 hour

Servings: 8

Ingredients:

6 rhubarb stalks, peeled and sliced
1 pound fresh strawberries, halved
3 tablespoons raw honey
1 teaspoon lemon zest
1 teaspoon orange zest
1 cup whole wheat flour

1 cup almond flour
¼ cup coconut oil, melted
2 tablespoons maple syrup
½ cup sliced almonds

Directions:

Combine the rhubarb, strawberries, honey, lemon zest and orange zest in a deep dish baking pan.

For the topping, mix the flours, coconut oil and maple syrup in a bowl. Mix well then spread the mixture over the fruits.

Top with sliced almonds and bake in the preheated oven at 350F for 40 minutes or until golden brown.

Serve the pie chilled.

Nutritional information per serving

Calories: 234
Fat: 11.9g

Protein: 4.4g
Carbohydrates: 30.0g

GRILLED PEACHES WITH YOGURT

Time: 25 minutes

Servings: 4

Ingredients:

2 large peaches, halved and pitted
2 tablespoons raw honey
½ teaspoon cinnamon powder

1 cup low fat plain yogurt
¼ cup sliced almonds

Directions:

Drizzle the peach halves with honey and sprinkle with cinnamon powder.

Heat a grill pan over medium flame and place the peaches on the grill.

Cook until browned then place on serving plates.

Top with yogurt and almond slices and serve right away.

Nutritional information per serving

Calories: 132
Fat: 3.8g

Protein: 5.0g
Carbohydrates: 21.9g

MINTY WATERMELON POPSICLES

Time: 4 hours

Servings: 6

Ingredients:

4 cups seedless watermelon
4 mint leaves
1 lime, juiced

2 tablespoons raw honey
1 teaspoon lemon zest

Directions:

Combine all the ingredients in a blender and pulse until smooth.

Pour the mixture in a popsicle mold and freeze at least 3 hours.

When done, dip into hot water for a few seconds to unmold them easier.

Serve right away.

Nutritional information per serving

Calories: 59
Fat: 0.2g

Protein: 0.9g
Carbohydrates: 15.2g

GINGER PUMPKIN FLAN

Time: 1 hour

Servings: 6

Ingredients:

1½ cups pumpkin puree
½ cup sweetened condensed milk
4 egg yolks
1 egg

1 cup low fat milk
1 pinch salt
1 teaspoon grated ginger
1 teaspoon vanilla extract

Directions:

Combine all the ingredients in a bowl and mix well.
Pour the mixture in a deep dish baking pan and place the pan inside a larger one.
Pour hot water in the bigger pan and bake in the preheated oven at 330F for 35 minutes.
Serve the pumpkin flan chilled.

Nutritional information per serving

Calories: 169
Fat: 6.5g

Protein: 6.8g
Carbohydrates: 21.6g

APRICOT GALETTE

Time: 45 minutes

Servings: 6

Ingredients:

1½ cups whole wheat flour
1 pinch salt
¼ teaspoon baking powder
½ cup coconut oil, melted

2 tablespoons cold water
1½ pounds apricots, halved
3 tablespoons raw honey
½ teaspoon cinnamon powder

Directions:

Mix the flour, salt, baking powder, oil and cold water in a bowl and mix until a dough begins to form.
Transfer the mix to a floured working surface and knead it quickly to form it into a dough.
Roll the dough into a thin round.
Place the apricots in the center of the dough and drizzle with honey. Sprinkle with cinnamon then wrap the edges of the dough over the apricots, leaving the center exposed.
Bake in the preheated oven at 350F for 30 minutes.
Serve the galette chilled.

Nutritional information per serving

Calories: 357
Fat: 19.2g

Protein: 4.7g
Carbohydrates: 45.0g

Orange Parfait

Time: 1 hour

Servings: 4

Ingredients:

2 oranges, cut into segments
1 teaspoon orange zest
1 cup low fat yogurt

2 tablespoons cream cheese
2 tablespoons raw honey
½ teaspoon vanilla extract

Directions:

Combine all the ingredients in a blender and pulse until smooth.
Pour the mixture in an ice cream machine and churn according to your machine's instructions.
Serve the parfait right away or store in an airtight container.

Nutritional information per serving

Calories: 138
Fat: 2.6g

Protein: 4.8g
Carbohydrates: 24.1g

Moroccan Spiced Orange Salad

Time: 35 minutes

Servings: 4

Ingredients:

6 oranges, cut into segments
1 teaspoon lemon juice
¼ teaspoon cinnamon powder

¼ teaspoon ground ginger
1 teaspoon orange zest
2 tablespoons sliced almonds

Directions:

Combine the orange segments, lemon juice, cinnamon, ginger, orange zest and almonds in a bowl.
Serve the salad right away.

Nutritional information per serving

Calories: 148
Fat: 1.8g

Protein: 3.2g
Carbohydrates: 33.3g

Cherry Almond Crisp

Time: 1 hour

Servings: 10

Ingredients:

Filling:
2 pounds cherries, pitted
1 tablespoon cornstarch

3 tablespoons raw honey
2 mint leaves, chopped
1 pinch cinnamon powder

Topping:

1½ pounds whole wheat flour
½ cup rolled oats

¼ cup sliced almonds
2 tablespoons raw honey
¼ cup coconut oil, melted

Directions:

For the filling, combine all the ingredients in a deep dish baking pan.

For the topping, combine the wheat flour, oats, almonds, honey and oil in a bowl and mix well until grainy.

Spread the mixture over the cherries and bake in the preheated oven at 350F for 35-40 minutes or until golden brown.

Serve the crisp chilled.

Nutritional information per serving

Calories: 464
Fat: 7.7g

Protein: 8.5g
Carbohydrates: 90.2g

Baked Buttermilk Custard

Time: 1 hour

Servings: 6

Ingredients:

2 cups buttermilk
2 egg yolks
2 whole eggs
3 tablespoons raw honey

1 cup low fat milk
1 teaspoon vanilla extract
1 teaspoon lemon zest
1 pinch salt

Directions:

Combine all the ingredients in a bowl and mix well.

Pour the mixture into a deep dish baking pan and bake in the preheated oven at 350F for 30 minutes.

Serve the custard chilled.

Nutritional information per serving

Calories: 123
Fat: 4.1g

Protein: 6.9g
Carbohydrates: 15.1g

Amaretto Baked Pears

Time: 45 minutes

Servings: 4

Ingredients:

2 large pears
4 tablespoons Amaretto
1 cup apple juice
1 star anise
1 cinnamon stick

2 whole cloves
2 tablespoons raw honey

Directions:

Peel the pears and cut them in half. Carefully remove the core and place the pears in a deep dish baking pan. Add the rest of the ingredients and cook in the preheated oven at 350F for 30-35 minutes.
Serve the pears chilled.

Nutritional information per serving

Calories: 173
Fat: 0.5g

Protein: 0.6g
Carbohydrates: 33.1g

Tapioca Pudding with Crushed Berry Sauce

Time: 40 minutes

Servings: 4

Ingredients:

½ cup tapioca pearls
1 cup coconut milk
1 cup water
3 tablespoons raw honey
½ teaspoon vanilla extract

1 cup raspberries
½ cup blueberries
1 teaspoon lemon juice
2 tablespoons maple syrup

Directions:

Combine the tapioca pearls, coconut milk, water, honey and vanilla in a saucepan.
Cook on low heat for 25 minutes.
Spoon the pudding into serving glasses and allow to cool down.
For the sauce, crush the berries in a bowl with the lemon juice and maple syrup.
Top the pudding with the crushed berry sauce and serve right away.

Nutritional information per serving

Calories: 285
Fat: 14.6g

Protein: 2.0g
Carbohydrates: 40.7g

Gingery Baked Apples

Time: 50 minutes

Servings: 6

Ingredients:

6 green apples
3 tablespoons maple syrup
1 teaspoon grated ginger

½ cup raisins
2 tablespoons dried cranberries
1 cup water

Directions:

Carefully remove the core of each apple and place them in a baking tray.
Mix the maple syrup, ginger, raisins and cranberries in a bowl.
Stuff each apple with the raisin mixture then pour in the water.
Cook in the preheated oven at 350F for 30 minutes.

Serve the apples chilled.

Nutritional information per serving

Calories: 159
Fat: 0.4g

Protein: 0.9g
Carbohydrates: 41.8g

ED PLUM CLAFOUTIS

Time: 45 minutes

Servings: 8

Ingredients:

1½ pounds red plums, halved and pitted
3 eggs
2 cups low fat milk

½ cup almond flour
1 pinch salt
½ teaspoon vanilla extract

Directions:

Place the red plums in a deep dish baking tray.
Mix the eggs, milk, almond flour, salt and vanilla in a bowl.
Pour the mixture over the plums and bake in the preheated oven at 350F for 30 minutes.
Serve the clafoutis chilled.

Nutritional information per serving

Calories: 85
Fat: 3.3g

Protein: 4.9g
Carbohydrates: 10.0g

ERRY BAKE

Time: 50 minutes

Servings: 8

Ingredients:

2 cups mixed berries
1 tablespoon cornstarch
½ cup coconut oil
¼ cup light brown sugar
2 eggs

1 cup low fat yogurt
1 teaspoon lemon zest
1 cup all-purpose flour
1 teaspoon baking powder
¼ teaspoon salt

Directions:

Mix the berries and cornstarch in a deep dish baking pan.
Mix the coconut oil, sugar and eggs in a bowl until creamy. Stir in the yogurt and lemon zest.
Add the flour, baking powder and salt then spoon the batter over the berries.
Bake in the preheated oven at 350F for 35-40 minutes until golden brown and fragrant.
Serve the bake chilled.

Nutritional information per serving

Calories: 254
Fat: 15.4g

Protein: 5.0g
Carbohydrates: 24.1g

Lemongrass Infused Tropical Compote

Time: 45 minutes

Servings: 4

Ingredients:

1 mango, peeled and sliced
1 pineapple, peeled and sliced
1 papaya, peeled and cubed
2 tablespoons coconut sugar

2 cups coconut water
2 lemongrass stalks, crushed
1 lime, sliced

Directions:

Combine all the ingredients in a saucepan.
Cover with a lid and cook on low heat for 20 minutes.
Allow the compote to cool down before serving.

Nutritional information per serving

Calories: 231
Fat: 1g

Protein: 1g
Carbohydrates: 11.5g

Apple Pear Cherry Compote

Time: 45 minutes

Servings: 8

Ingredients:

2 red apples, peeled and cored then sliced
2 pears, cored and sliced
1 pound dark cherries, pitted

1 star anise
2 cups water
1 teaspoon lemon juice

Directions:

Combine all the ingredients in a saucepan.
Cook on low heat for 20 minutes until softened.
Serve the compote chilled.

Nutritional information per serving

Calories: 353
Fat: 17.2g

Protein: 4.6g
Carbohydrates: 45.6g

Raspberry Banana Ice Cream

Time: 2 hours

Servings: 6

Ingredients:

4 bananas, sliced
1 cup frozen raspberries
2 tablespoons raw honey

½ cup coconut cream
½ teaspoon vanilla extract

Directions:

Place the banana slices in a tray and freeze them for at least 1½ hours.

When the bananas are frozen, place them in a food processor together with the rest of the ingredients.

Pulse until smooth and creamy.

Serve the ice cream right away or store in an airtight container in the freezer.

Nutritional information per serving

Calories: 181

Fat: 5.1g

Protein: 1.6g

Carbohydrates: 35.8g

Cinnamon Wild Rice Pudding

Time: 35 minutes

Servings: 6

Ingredients:

¾ cup wild rice

¼ cup rolled oats

1 cup coconut milk

1 cup water

1 cinnamon stick

1 star anise

3 tablespoons raw honey

Directions:

Combine the rice, oats, coconut milk, water, cinnamon and star anise in a saucepan.

Place on low heat and cook until the liquid is completely absorbed.

Remove from heat and add the honey.

Mix well and serve the pudding either warm or chilled.

Nutritional information per serving

Calories: 208

Fat: 10.0g

Protein: 4.4g

Carbohydrates: 28.2g

Chickpea Chocolate Cake

Time: 1 hour

Servings: 10

Ingredients:

2 cups canned chickpeas, drained

4 eggs

1½ cups dark chocolate chips, melted

1 teaspoon vanilla extract

1 pinch salt

Directions:

Place the chickpeas and eggs in a food processor and pulse until well mixed.

Add the melted chocolate, vanilla and salt and mix well.

Spoon the batter in a round cake pan lined with baking paper and bake in the preheated oven at 350F for 35-40 minutes.

When done, remove from the oven and allow to cool down then slice and serve.

Nutritional information per serving

Calories: 256
Fat: 9.0g

Protein: 11.1g
Carbohydrates: 36.5g

Lemon Polenta Cake

Time: 1 hour

Servings: 10

Ingredients:

1 cup polenta flour
1½ cups almond flour
1 teaspoon baking powder
½ teaspoon baking soda
½ teaspoon salt
½ cup raw honey

3 eggs
1 teaspoon lemon zest
1 teaspoon orange zest
1 teaspoon vanilla extract
2 tablespoons lemon juice

Directions:

In a bowl, combine the polenta flour, almond flour, baking powder, baking soda and salt.
In another bowl, mix the honey, eggs, lemon zest, orange zest, vanilla extract and lemon juice.
Pour the wet ingredients over the dry ones and give it a quick mix.
Pour the batter in a round cake pan lined with baking paper.
Bake in the preheated oven at 350F for 35-40 minutes or until well risen and golden brown.
Allow the cake to cool down then cut the cake into slices and serve.

Nutritional information per serving

Calories: 149
Fat: 3.4g

Protein: 3.8g
Carbohydrates: 26.2g

Raw Berry Pudding

Time: 15 minutes

Servings: 4

Ingredients:

2 cups fresh strawberries
½ cup fresh blueberries
3 tablespoons chia seeds

2 tablespoons agave syrup
½ teaspoon vanilla extract
1 teaspoon lemon juice

Directions:

Combine all the ingredients in a food processor.
Pulse until smooth then pour into serving glasses.
Allow to rest for 10 minutes then serve.

Nutritional information per serving

Calories: 184
Fat: 7.5g

Protein: 5.4g
Carbohydrates: 24.5g

ALMOND HONEY CAKE

Time: 1 hour

Servings: 8

Ingredients:

1½ cups almond flour
1 teaspoon baking soda
4 eggs, separated
¼ cup raw honey

1 teaspoon vanilla extract
½ teaspoon salt
½ cup almond slices

Directions:

Mix the almond flour with baking soda in a bowl and place aside.
Mix the egg yolks with honey until creamy and pale.
Stir in the vanilla and mix well.
In another bowl, whip the egg whites with a pinch of salt until fluffy.
Fold the whites into the egg yolk mixture, alternating with almond flour.
Pour the batter in a 9-inch round cake pan lined with baking paper. Top with almond slices.
Bake in the preheated oven at 350F for 35 minutes.
Allow the cake to cool in the pan before slicing and serving.

Nutritional information per serving

Calories: 118
Fat: 6.7g

Protein: 4.7g
Carbohydrates: 10.9g

HEALTHY AND DELICIOUS CHOCOLATE MOUSSE

Time: 15 minutes

Servings: 4

Ingredients:

2 ripe bananas
1 avocado, peeled and pitted
4 Medjool dates
2 tablespoons almond butter

2 tablespoons almond milk
2 tablespoons cocoa powder
1 tablespoon raw honey
1 pinch salt

Directions:

Combine all the ingredients in a food processor and pulse until smooth.
Spoon the mousse into serving glasses and serve right away.

Nutritional information per serving

Calories: 245
Fat: 16.7g

Protein: 4.0g
Carbohydrates: 25.4g

Strawberry Chia Pudding

Time: 20 minutes

Servings: 4

Ingredients:

¼ cup chia seeds
2 cups fresh strawberries
1 cup coconut milk

½ cup coconut water
2 tablespoons raw honey
1 teaspoon vanilla extract

Directions:

Combine all the ingredients in a blender and pulse until smooth.
Pour the mixture in serving glasses and serve after 10 minutes.

Nutritional information per serving

Calories: 211
Fat: 15.2g

Protein: 2.5g
Carbohydrates: 19.4g

Cardamom Tapioca Pudding

Time: 35 minutes

Servings: 4

Ingredients:

½ cup tapioca pearls
1 cup coconut milk
1 cup water

4 cardamom pods, crushed
3 tablespoons maple syrup
1 pinch salt

Directions:

Combine the tapioca pearls, coconut milk, water, cardamom, maple syrup and salt in a saucepan.
Place over low heat and cook for 20-25 minutes until thickened.
Spoon the pudding into serving glasses and serve the pudding chilled.

Nutritional information per serving

Calories: 228
Fat: 14.5g

Protein: 1.6g
Carbohydrates: 26.0g

Caramelized Pineapple

Time: 20 minutes

Servings: 4

Ingredients:

4 pineapple slices
2 tablespoons raw honey
1 lime, juiced
1 teaspoon lime zest

Directions:

Combine all the ingredients in a bowl and toss around until evenly coated.
Heat a grill pan over medium flame and place the pineapple on the grill, preserving the sauce in the bowl.
Cook on each side for 2-3 minutes until browned.
Serve the pineapple fresh, drizzled with the sauce left in the bowl.

Nutritional information per serving

Calories: 161
Fat: 0.3g

Protein: 1.5g
Carbohydrates: 43.3g

Mango Gratin

Time: 20 minutes   Servings: 2

Ingredients:

1 ripe mango, peeled and sliced
Zest and juice of 1 lime
2 tablespoons maple syrup   ½ cup low fat yogurt

Directions:

Mix the mango, lime zest and lime juice in a bowl. Add the maple syrup and mix well.
Heat a grill pan over medium flame and place the mango on the grill.
Cook on each side until golden brown.
Remove from heat and serve the mango topped with yogurt.

Nutritional information per serving

Calories: 168
Fat: 1.1g

Protein: 4.0g
Carbohydrates: 35.3g

Tropical Popsicles

Time: 3 hours   Servings: 6

Ingredients:

2 bananas   1 teaspoon lemon juice
1 mango, peeled and sliced   2 tablespoons maple syrup
1 cup coconut milk   ½ teaspoon vanilla extract
1 cup coconut water

Directions:

Combine all the ingredients in blender and pulse until smooth and creamy.
Pour the mixture in a popsicle mold and freeze for at least 2 hours.
When done, dip the popsicle mold into hot water for a few seconds to unmold them easier.
Serve right away.

Nutritional information per serving

Calories: 177
Fat: 9.9g

Protein: 1.8g
Carbohydrates: 23.1g

ANFORTE

Time: 1 hour

Servings: 8

Ingredients:

1 cup hazelnuts
1 cup almonds
6 oz. dried figs
2 oz. candied orange peel
½ cup sorghum flour
½ cup tapioca flour

2 tablespoons cocoa powder
¼ teaspoon cinnamon powder
½ teaspoon ground ginger
¼ teaspoon ground coriander
½ cup raw honey
½ cup fresh orange juice

Directions:

Place the hazelnuts and almonds in a food processor and pulse until ground.
Add the rest of the ingredients and mix well.
Spoon the mixture into a small round cake pan and press it well on the bottom of the pan.
Bake in the preheated oven at 350F for 20 minutes.
Allow to cool down before slicing and serving.

Nutritional information per serving

Calories: 305
Fat: 12.5g

Protein: 6.5g
Carbohydrates: 48.7g

QUINOA APPLE RAISIN CAKE

Time: 1 hour

Servings: 8

Ingredients:

1 ½ cups cooked quinoa
½ cup coconut oil, melted
2 eggs
½ cup maple syrup
1 cup golden raisins
2 apples, peeled, cored and diced

1 cup whole wheat flour
1 teaspoon baking powder
½ teaspoon baking soda
½ teaspoon cinnamon powder
¼ teaspoon ground ginger

Directions:

Combine the quinoa, coconut oil, eggs, maple syrup, raisins and apples in a bowl.
Stir in the remaining ingredients and mix well.
Spoon the batter in a 9-inch round cake pan lined with baking paper.
Bake the cake in the preheated oven at 350F for 30 minutes.
Allow the cake to cool down before slicing and serving.

Nutritional information per serving

Calories: 438
Fat: 17.0g

Protein: 8.2g
Carbohydrates: 66.7g

Chocolate Avocado Cake

Time: 50 minutes

Servings: 8

Ingredients:

1 avocado, peeled and pitted
¼ cup raw honey
4 eggs
1 teaspoon vanilla extract
¼ teaspoon cinnamon powder
½ teaspoon baking soda

½ cup cocoa powder
½ cup tapioca flour
½ cup sorghum flour
¼ cup coconut flour
½ teaspoon salt

Directions:

Mix the avocado, honey, eggs and vanilla in a food processor and pulse until smooth.
Add the rest of the ingredients and mix well.
Spoon the batter in a 9-inch round cake and bake in the preheated oven at 350F for 35 minutes.
Allow the cake to cool down then slice and serve.

Nutritional information per serving

Calories: 186
Fat: 8.7g

Protein: 6.1g
Carbohydrates: 25.5g

Raspberry Muffins

Time: 50 minutes

Servings: 12

Ingredients:

5 egg whites
3 tablespoons raw honey
1 teaspoon vanilla extract
1 cup low fat yogurt
¼ cup coconut oil, melted

1 cup whole wheat flour
1 teaspoon baking powder
¼ teaspoon salt
1 cup fresh raspberries

Directions:

Mix the egg whites, honey, vanilla, yogurt and coconut oil in a bowl.
Stir in the flour, baking powder and salt and mix quickly.
Fold in the raspberries then spoon the batter in a muffin tin lined with muffin papers.
Bake in the preheated oven at 350F for 20 minutes.
Allow the muffins to cool down before serving.

Nutritional information per serving

Calories: 121
Fat: 5.0g

Protein: 3.9g
Carbohydrates: 15.3g

ANANA BREAD

Time: 1 hour

Servings: 10

Ingredients:

2 bananas, mashed
2 eggs
1 cup low fat milk
¼ cup raw honey
1 cup whole wheat flour
1 cup rolled oats

1 teaspoon baking soda
1 teaspoon baking powder
½ teaspoon salt
1 teaspoon pumpkin spice mix
¼ cup dried cranberries

Directions:

Mix the bananas, eggs, milk and honey in a bowl.
Stir in the flour, oats, baking soda, baking powder, salt and spice and mix well.
Fold in the cranberries then spoon the batter in a loaf cake pan lined with baking paper.
Bake in the preheated oven at 350F for 30-40 minutes or until golden brown.
Serve the bread chilled.

Nutritional information per serving

Calories: 158
Fat: 1.8g

Protein: 4.6g
Carbohydrates: 31.5g

THYME PEACH CRUMBLE

Time: 1 hour

Servings: 8

Ingredients:

2 pounds peaches, pitted and sliced
1 teaspoon dried thyme
1 lemon, zested and juiced
2 tablespoons agave syrup

1 cup whole wheat flour
½ cup rolled oats
¼ cup coconut oil, melted
1 pinch salt

Directions:

Mix the peaches, thyme, lemon zest, lemon juice and agave syrup in a deep dish baking pan.
For the topping, put the flour, oats, coconut oil and salt in a bowl and mix well.
Spread the mixture over the peaches and bake in the preheated oven at 350F for 40 minutes.
Serve the crumble chilled.

Nutritional information per serving

Calories: 198
Fat: 7.6g

Protein: 3.4g
Carbohydrates: 31.2g

CHERRY RICOTTA PARFAIT

Time: 20 minutes

Servings: 4

Ingredients:

2 cups cherries, pitted
½ cup water
2 tablespoons raw honey

1 mint leaf
2 cups ricotta cheese

Directions:

Combine the cherries, water, honey and mint in a saucepan and cook on low heat for 5 minutes.
Spoon the ricotta cheese into serving glasses.
Top with cherries and serve right away.

Nutritional information per serving

Calories: 252
Fat: 10.2g

Protein: 14.4g
Carbohydrates: 26.1g

BANANA COOKIES

Time: 45 minutes

Servings: 20

Ingredients:

4 bananas, mashed
½ cup dates, pitted
¼ cup coconut oil, melted

2 cups rolled oats
1 teaspoon baking soda
¼ teaspoon salt

Directions:

Combine the bananas, dates and coconut oil in a blender and pulse until smooth.
Fold in the oats, baking soda and salt then spoon the batter on a baking tray lined with baking paper.
Bake in the preheated oven at 350F for 20 minutes.
Allow the cookies to cool down before serving or storing.

Nutritional information per serving

Calories: 88
Fat: 3.4g

Protein: 1.5g
Carbohydrates: 14.3g

DARK CHERRY CLAFOUTI

Time: 45 minutes

Servings: 8

Ingredients:

3 cups dark cherries, pitted
4 eggs

1½ cups low fat milk
¼ cup coconut oil, melted

1 teaspoon vanilla extract
¼ cup maple syrup
¾ cup almond flour

1 teaspoon lemon zest

Directions:

Place the cherries on the bottom of a round baking pan greased with coconut oil.
Mix the eggs, milk, coconut oil, vanilla, maple syrup and lemon zest, as well as almond flour in a bowl.
Pour the mixture over the cherries and bake in the preheated oven at 350F for 30 minutes.
Serve the clafouti chilled.

Nutritional information per serving

Calories: 231
Fat: 15.3g

Protein: 6.0g
Carbohydrates: 18.0g

Banana Peach Frozen Dessert

Time: 2 hours

Servings: 4

Ingredients:

2 bananas
2 peaches, pitted
1 cup cashew nuts, soaked overnight
½ cup coconut water

1 teaspoon lemon juice
2 tablespoons raw honey
½ teaspoon vanilla extract

Directions:

Combine all the ingredients in a food processor and pulse until smooth and creamy.
Pour the mixture in an ice cream machine and churn according to your machine's instructions.
Serve right away or store in an airtight container in the freezer.

Nutritional information per serving

Calories: 308
Fat: 16.2g

Protein: 6.6g
Carbohydrates: 39.2g

Apricot Cobbler

Time: 1 hour

Servings: 8

Ingredients:

2 pounds apricots, pitted
3 tablespoons maple syrup
½ teaspoon cinnamon powder
1 cup whole wheat flour
½ cup rolled oats

1 cup coconut milk
½ cup water
1 teaspoon baking soda
¼ teaspoon salt
¼ cup sliced almonds

Directions:

Mix the apricots, maple syrup and cinnamon in a deep dish baking pan.
For the topping, mix the flour, oats, coconut milk, water, baking soda and salt in a bowl.
Spoon the batter over the apricots and top with sliced almonds.
Bake in the preheated oven at 350F for 35-40 minutes or until well risen and golden brown.
Serve the cobbler chilled.

Nutritional information per serving

Calories: 236
Fat: 9.9g

Protein: 5.1g
Carbohydrates: 35.2g

Pear Sorbet

Time: 2 hours

Servings: 8

Ingredients:

4 pears, peeled and cored
½ teaspoon vanilla extract

¼ cup maple syrup
2 cups water

Directions:

Combine all the ingredients in a saucepan and cook on low heat for 20 minutes.
Remove from heat and allow to cool down then puree the mix with an immersion blender.
Pour the mixture in an ice cream machine and churn according to your machine's instructions.
Serve the sorbet right away or store in an airtight container in the freezer.

Nutritional information per serving

Calories: 87
Fat: 0.2g

Protein: 0.4g
Carbohydrates: 22.5g

Pear Upside Down Cake

Time: 1 hour

Servings: 8

Ingredients:

3 pears, peeled and sliced
½ cup coconut oil, softened
¼ cup maple syrup
2 eggs
4 egg yolks
½ cup water

1½ cups whole wheat flour
½ cup polenta flour
½ teaspoon salt
1 teaspoon baking powder
¼ teaspoon baking soda

Directions:

Place the pear slices at the bottom of a round cake pan lined with baking paper.
Mix the coconut oil, maple syrup, eggs, egg yolks and water in a bowl.
Stir in the flours, salt, baking powder and baking soda and mix well.

Spoon the batter over the pear slices and bake in the preheated oven at 350F for 35-40 minutes or until golden brown and well risen.

Allow the cake to cool down before serving.

Nutritional information per serving

Calories: 350

Fat: 17.3g

Protein: 6.2g

Carbohydrates: 43.9g

LEMON PANNA COTTA

Time: 1½ hours

Servings: 4

Ingredients:

1 teaspoon gelatin powder

2 tablespoons cold water

1 cup plain yogurt

1 cup low fat milk

2 tablespoons lemon juice

2 teaspoons lemon zest

3 tablespoons raw honey

Fresh blueberries for serving

Directions:

Bloom the gelatin in cold water in a bowl.

In another bowl, mix the yogurt, milk, lemon juice and lemon zest. Add the honey as well then melt the gelatin and stir it into the mixture.

Pour the panna cotta into 4 serving glasses and allow to set in the fridge.

Serve the panna cotta topped with fresh blueberries.

Nutritional information per serving

Calories: 135

Fat: 1.5g

Protein: 7.3g

Carbohydrates: 23.2g

CHIA COCONUT PUDDING

Time: 35 minutes

Servings: 4

Ingredients:

1 cup coconut milk

1 cup water

3 tablespoons agave syrup

4 tablespoons chia seeds

½ teaspoon vanilla extract

Directions:

Combine all the ingredients in a bowl.

Pour the mixture into serving glasses and place in the fridge for 20 minutes.

Serve the pudding chilled.

Nutritional information per serving

Calories: 343

Fat: 23.9g

Protein: 7.7g

Carbohydrates: 26.5g

BAKED PEACHES WITH RICOTTA CHEESE

Time: 30 minutes   Servings: 4

Ingredients:

2 peaches, halved and pitted   ½ teaspoon ground ginger
2 tablespoons maple syrup   1 cup ricotta cheese
½ teaspoon cinnamon powder

Directions:

Place the peach halves on a baking tray lined with baking paper.
Drizzle the peaches with maple syrup and sprinkle with cinnamon and ginger.
Place a dollop of ricotta cheese on top of each peach half and bake in the preheated oven at 350F for 15 minutes.
Serve the peaches warm or chilled.

Nutritional information per serving

Calories: 132   Protein: 7.5g
Fat: 5.1g   Carbohydrates: 14.7g

BANANA ALMOND FRITTERS

Time: 35 minutes   Servings: 2

Ingredients:

2 bananas, mashed   1 egg
½ cup almond flour   2 tablespoons coconut oil, melted
1 tablespoon maple syrup

Directions:

Mix all the ingredients in a bowl.
Heat a non-stick pan over medium flame and drop spoonfuls of batter on the hot pan.
Fry on each side for 1-2 minutes until golden brown.
Serve the fritters warm.

Nutritional information per serving

Calories: 320   Protein: 5.6g
Fat: 19.7g   Carbohydrates: 35g

*F*LOURLESS CHOCOLATE ORANGE CAKE

Time: 1½ hours

Servings: 8

Ingredients:

2 oranges
2 eggs
¼ cup raw honey
¼ cup cocoa powder

1 cup almond flour
¼ teaspoon baking powder
1 pinch salt

Directions:

Place the oranges in a saucepan and cover with water. Cook on low heat for 30 minutes.
When done, remove from the water and place in a food processor. Pulse until smooth then add the eggs and honey. Mix well.
Stir in the cocoa powder, almond flour, baking powder and salt.
Pour the batter in an 8-inch round cake pan lined with baking paper.
Bake in the preheated oven at 350F for 40 minutes.
Serve the cake chilled.

Nutritional information per serving

Calories: 96
Fat: 3.2g

Protein: 3.1g
Carbohydrates: 16.5g

*F*RUIT SALAD WITH MINTED DRESSING

Time: 30 minutes

Servings: 4

Ingredients:

4 kiwi fruits, peeled and sliced
2 oranges, cut into segments
2 grapefruits, cut into segments
2 pears, peeled and sliced
2 bananas, sliced

½ cup fresh blueberries
½ cup plain yogurt
6 mint leaves, chopped
2 tablespoons raw honey
1 teaspoon lemon zest

Directions:

Mix the kiwi fruits, oranges, grapefruits, pears, bananas and blueberries in a salad bowl.
For the dressing, mix the yogurt, mint, honey and lemon zest in a bowl.
Top the salad with the dressing and serve right away.

Nutritional information per serving

Calories: 287
Fat: 1.3g

Protein: 5.1g
Carbohydrates: 70g

$\mathcal{P}$UMPKIN CHOCOLATE COOKIES

Time: 45 minutes

Servings: 20

Ingredients:

1 cup rolled oats
½ cup whole wheat flour
¼ teaspoon cinnamon powder
2 tablespoons cocoa powder
¼ teaspoon baking soda

¼ teaspoon salt
½ teaspoon ground ginger
1 cup canned pumpkin
¼ cup water
2 tablespoons coconut oil, melted

Directions:

Mix the oats, flour, cinnamon, cocoa powder, baking soda, salt and ginger in a bowl.
Add the pumpkin, water and coconut oil and mix well.
Drop spoonfuls of batter on a baking tray lined with parchment paper.
Bake in the preheated oven at 350F for 15-20 minutes or until golden brown and fragrant.
Allow to cool down before serving.

Nutritional information per serving

Calories: 44
Fat: 1.8g

Protein: 1.1g
Carbohydrates: 6.5g

$\mathcal{A}$VOCADO CHOCOLATE BREAD

Time: 1 hour

Servings: 10

Ingredients:

1 avocado, mashed
4 tablespoons coconut oil, melted
½ teaspoon vanilla extract
½ cup coconut milk
3 tablespoons raw honey
2 eggs

2 cups almond flour
¼ cup cocoa powder
1 teaspoon baking soda
¼ teaspoon salt
½ cup pecans, chopped

Directions:

Mix the avocado, coconut oil, vanilla, coconut milk, honey and eggs in a bowl.
Add the rest of the ingredients and mix well.
Spoon the batter in a loaf cake pan lined with baking paper.
Bake in the preheated oven at 350F for 40 minutes.
Allow the cake to cool down before slicing and serving.

Nutritional information per serving

Calories: 173
Fat: 14.4g

Protein: 2.5g
Carbohydrates: 8.9g

CONCLUSION

Eating healthy is not just a trend. There's clear medical evidence of how diets influence our lives. That's precisely why we need to focus on clean ingredients and foods rather than fast food or ready-made supermarket dishes. Because if we don't, we face serious consequences – health problems, fatigue, dull skin and hair, lack of energy to do even the simplest of things. And if there's one thing I learned over the years, that's taking care of myself – because no one else does it and definitely the food industry doesn't care how well I am or how long I live. So it's time for a change – now, not tomorrow or the day after that, but now! Choose clean eating and get back your well-being! Make a change to the best for your own sake!

Thank you again for purchasing this book!

Finally, if you enjoyed this book, please take the time to share your thoughts and post a review on Amazon. It'd be greatly appreciated!

Feel free to contact me at emma.katie@outlook.com

Check out more books by Emma Katie at:

www.amazon.com/author/emmakatie

CPSIA information can be obtained
at www.ICGtesting.com
Printed in the USA
LVOW09s1652171117

556714LV00001B/4/P